Paul and Me

Also by A. E. Hotchner

Paul and Me

✦ ✦ ✦ ✦ ✦

Paul and Me

❖ ❖ ❖ ❖ ❖

Fifty-three Years of

Adventures and Misadventures with My Pal

Paul Newman

A. E. Hotchner

SIMON &
SCHUSTER

London · New York · Sydney · Toronto

A CBS COMPANY

First published in Great Britain in 2010 by Simon & Schuster UK Ltd
A CBS COMPANY

Grateful acknowledgement is made to Notable Music for permission to reprint
the lyrics for 'If There Were More People Like You' by Dorothy Fields.
Reprinted by permission of Notable Music.

1 3 5 7 9 10 8 6 4 2

Simon & Schuster UK Ltd
1st Floor
222 Gray's Inn Road
London
WC1X 8HB

www.simonandschuster.co.uk

Simon & Schuster Australia
Sydney

A CIP catalogue copy for this book is available
from the British Library.

ISBN: 978-1-84737-783-8 (hardback)
ISBN: 978-1-84737-784-5 (trade paperback)

Printed in the UK by CPI Mackays, Chatham ME5 8TD
Designed by Maria Carella

For Paul

NOTE TO THE READER

Some of the fifty-three years of our friendship was involved in starting Newman's Own and the Hole in the Wall Gang camps, and I have recounted that in this memoir.

Several years ago, Paul and I wrote a slim business book called *Shameless Exploitation in Pursuit of the Common Good*, which turned out to be one of our major misadventures. To those few who happened to have read it, I hope they will indulge the passages that have found their way into this book in the context of our friendship.

A.E.H.

Paul and Me

◆ ◆ ◆ ◆ ◆

Up Front

Paul Newman was an unadorned man. He was direct and honest and off-center and mischievous and romantic and very handsome. All of these attributes became the generating force behind him. He was the same man in 2008 that he was in 1955, unchanged despite all the honors and the fame, not a whisper of a change. That was something—the constancy of the man.

In these bleak times that feature men whose greed and selfishness have been so disillusioning and ruinous to their fellow citizens, Paul's concern for those less fortunate and his altruistic mien were important antidotes.

He was a complicated, unpredictable, talented man who certainly gave back to the world as much as the world gave to him.

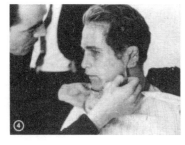

AN EMBATTLED ACTOR
AGES FAST

Paul Newman gains 20 years in one hour

Time rolled in reverse in last week's TV version of a famous Ernest Hemingway short story, *The Battler*. In 10-year leaps the story looked in on the life and times of a 40-year-old punch-drunk panhandler, who a decade earlier was an untameable tough in prison, and who at the age of 20 was a brash and unbeatable champion of the prize ring. An hour-long drama, produced by Fred Coe on NBC-TV's *Playwrights' '56* show, it gave Actor Paul Newman in the adaptation's title role an embattled night with the studio make-up artists.

Pictured here, as if the TV show were being played backward, Paul Newman in 1) is without much make-up, a 20-year-old on top of the fight game. In 2), during a 1½-minute break, he is having a 10-year alteration made on his face before he appears in 3) as a problem prisoner. In 4) another 10-year change is applied during the play's commercial to make the battler in 5) a pulp-faced, brainless old bum. Though it was not a very good night for Hemingway, it was a busy and effective night for Newman.

*P*aul Newman and I first met in 1955 in a funeral parlor on La Cienega Boulevard in Hollywood. There were sample coffins in the anteroom, but the large viewing room beyond had been stripped of its funereal paraphernalia and instead outfitted for the rehearsal of *The Battler*, a television drama I had written based on a Hemingway short story. It was my first television play and, as it turned out, it became a fortuitous launching pad for Paul's career as well as my own. We were in this mortuary because NBC had run out of rehearsal space, and this bizarre spot was the best they could do.

Both Paul and I were at the start of our respective careers and each of us had come to a halt. Paul had been brought up in Shaker Heights, an affluent suburb of Cleveland. He had been in a dozen or so plays at Kenyon College, and after graduation he had performed in summer stock—once playing the gentleman caller in Tennessee Williams's *The Glass Menagerie*. He later enrolled in Yale University School of Drama, where in Shaw's *Saint Joan* he was required to weep onstage. As Paul told me years later, "The muscles contracted in my stomach, and immediately I tried to figure out some way to play the whole thing facing upstage. And then I thought, What an ass. I drag my family—I had married an actress I had met when I was in Woodstock summer theater and had a son with her—with only nine hundred dollars in the bank, all the way to Connecticut, and then think of all the ways I can cop out. At the time I was living in a boardinghouse, and I took that script downstairs to the boiler room and I said, Okay buddy, you are going to sit here until you find out where it is going to come from or you get out of this business right now. I did the part and my tears arrived on cue."

After Yale he was accepted by the Actors Studio. Marlon Brando and James Dean were in his session, and they were given the leads in most of the scenes that were performed. Paul admitted he did not have the aggression that one needs to get noticed and also was terrible at sight-reading a new script. He and Dean performed together in a screen test for a part in *East of Eden*, and Dean got the part.

Paul picked up small parts in TV dramas that were being filmed in New York, and he landed a small part in *Picnic* on Broadway and was also the understudy to Ralph Meeker, who played the lead. Later in the run, when Meeker went on vacation, Newman asked the director, Josh Logan, if he could take Meeker's role when the play went on the road. But Logan told him no; he didn't think Paul carried enough "sexual threat."

As for me, I had come from the rough streets of Depression-era St. Louis, and had made my way through Washington University Law School and the air force. Rejecting the banality of lawyering, I had opted for freelance writing and was attempting to liberate myself from the dead end of magazine work. Years before, in 1948, I had visited Ernest Hemingway at his finca in Cuba to edit his novel *Across the River and into the Trees* for magazine serialization. At that time Hemingway was being pursued by television producers. "Hordes from the north," he said. "They sweep down like Huns with their deals and residuals." He felt "under siege" and, because I was from New York and he assumed I understood that world, he asked me if I would be willing to screen the "dross from the brass." I told him I would do what I could, but that I had never written for television and knew nothing about it. "That puts you a jump ahead of all those network geniuses who think they do," he replied.

This eventually led to my converting Hemingway's brief story "The Battler" into a television play. Fred Coe, the veteran producer, had cast an actor named Paul Newman to play a supporting role. Paul had recently appeared on Broadway as one of the hoods in *The Desperate Hours* and had acted in one film, *The Silver Chalice*, which had been a fiasco. When Coe asked him about *The Silver Chalice*, Paul blamed his agent, who had told him, "They've been knocking and knocking on your door, offering you scripts, but at some point they're just going to stop. And the trick is to answer the last knock before they quit." So when this awful script arrived, his agent said, "This may be the last knock," so Paul accepted. He said it "was without a doubt, the worst film made in the entire decade of the fifties."

The role Paul was to play in *The Battler* was that of Nick Adams, a teenager who runs away from home and encounters an addle-brained, psychopathic former boxing champ at a campsite alongside a railroad track. Although Paul was thirty-one years old, he had a youthfulness that allowed him to play much younger.

No sooner had the set builders and costume designers started work on *The Battler* than we got the tragic news that James Dean, who was to play Ad Francis, the battler, had died in an accident involving his souped-up sports car. Now, with rehearsals imminent, we were without a leading actor in this long and difficult part that called for a punch-drunk, dangerously unbalanced, suspicious ex-pug who was once welterweight champion of the world, a part that moved back in time, depicting the boxer in his prime. After a frantic search for a star to replace Dean on such short notice, Coe reluctantly turned to Paul, lamenting having to go with a relatively unknown actor in the demanding lead role.

The following day Coe, the director, Arthur Penn, and I met with Paul in Coe's office to tell him he was being recast. Paul was reluctant, not only about replacing his friend James Dean ("I don't want to take advantage of anyone else's misfortune") but because he was not sure he could handle the part. Coe and Penn spent the next half hour trying to convince Paul that the role was less demanding than he thought, but he remained hesitant. He said he wanted to reread the script and think about it.

This was a depressing unraveling of what had promised to be a play that would open a fresh career for me. The role that Paul was tentatively rejecting was, in my judgment, a great opportunity for an actor to make a name for himself. In a way, I admired Paul for his reticence, but I knew that if he rejected the part, the show would have to be canceled. And so would my hope of escaping from the confinement of magazine writing.

In the elevator after leaving Coe's office, I told Paul that I sympathized with his reluctance and suggested we talk about it.

"Sure," he said, "let's have a beer."

We settled into a booth at a nearby bar and grill and ordered Budweisers. "I know how you feel," I said. "When I was faced with having to turn Hemingway's short story into a full-length drama, my first try at playwriting, I didn't think it was possible. At least you bring some acting experience to the table."

"Yeah," he said, "but that's not saying much. Maybe I'm fooling myself. Maybe I need a new line of work. I guess it's too late to be a dentist."

I liked him. I was touched by his honesty. At that moment, apart from my desire to get the play performed, I truly felt he would have the perseverance to master the role. "Listen," I said, "we're both trying to get up and out. You from secondary, meaningless television roles. Me from magazines, like the "This Week" Sunday newspaper inserts and an occasional *Saturday Evening Post* article. I have a couple of kids, so do you, so we don't have a lot of loose time lying around. We could play it safe but we'd never make it. I believe in the dictum of that great philosopher, Babe Ruth, who said, 'Never let the fear of striking out get in your way.' " By that time I was ready for a Scotch and Newman decided to join me. He flagged the waitress. "Two Glenlivets and a couple of burgers, medium rare, okay?"

"Any way you want it, sweetheart," the waitress said.

When the waitress returned with the drinks, I asked her, "Do you think he's a sexual threat?"

"You betcha!" she said, and beamed at him.

I raised my glass. "Here's to the battler," I said.

He raised his. "Here's to Babe Ruth," he said.

DURING THE BEGINNING of rehearsals, Paul was out of sync, floundering, trying to discover something in himself that related to the character he was playing. In the story, this is how Hemingway had described the character: "His nose was sunken, his eyes were slits, he had queer-shaped lips . . . the man's face was queerly formed and mutilated. It was like putty in color . . . He had only one ear. It was thickened and tight against the side of his head. Where the other ear should have been, there was a stump."

I felt sorry for Paul because he had been talked into a part that he knew he wasn't suited for. Makeup could create the face, but he had to find some way to identify with this pathetic character who was totally foreign to him. Paul was hurting badly.

One day, after rehearsal ended and I was leaving through the casket room, a voice from one of the caskets called out, "Hotch!" I levitated and when I returned to terra firma I cautiously approached the casket. Paul was laid out, his arms folded across his chest. "Batten down the lid," he said. "I'm checking out."

I helped him out of the casket and we went to the bar and grill for a couple of beers. We didn't mention the play or the elusive battler who was bedeviling him. He simply wanted to take his mind off of the frustration of that day's rehearsal. The casket gambit was the kind of Newmanesque distraction that would take place numerous times over the coming years.

But one morning, as he started to rehearse a pivotal scene at the campsite, the slurred, halting speech, the stiff-legged shuffle, the jerks and twitches of a stumblebum prizefighter suddenly emerged. This accomplishment was not an accident. Paul had started to hang out at the YMCA, a run-down building in downtown Los Angeles next to the grubby gym where local boxers worked out. He had found a punch-drunk welterweight named Bobby Wilcox with whom he had become friends, and now Paul was slowly assuming the old pug's persona. It was a thrilling metamorphosis.

During our lunch break, it was customary for us to go to our diner where we sat in a booth and discussed the morning's work. Most of the time, a lovely young actress named Joanne Woodward came to join us. She had been in *Picnic* with Paul, and it was obvious that they were very much in love. They were a beautiful couple and they certainly illuminated the booth. Paul was still married, but it was apparent that in due time his entente with Joanne would replace the marriage.

By the time *The Battler* aired and was pictorially covered in *Life* magazine, Paul and I had become friends. MGM had been trying to cast Rocky Graziano's autobiography, *Somebody Up There Likes Me*, an account of his brutal life as welterweight champion. On the basis of his performance in *The Battler*, Paul was offered the part. For the second time, ironically, it was a part that had been intended for James Dean.

Paul called to tell me the good news and we had a congratulatory evening to celebrate both his good fortune and mine, for I had just signed a contract to write a play for *Playhouse 90*. In the course of that evening at The Brown Derby, Paul and I indulged in the irreverent, politically liberal, scatological, rebellious, ambitious, and irresponsible prejudices, ideas, and dreams that we shared.

As the night ended and we went our separate tipsy ways, we had solidified a comradery that was destined to keep us as closely bonded friends for the next fifty years.

I visited Paul on the set of *Somebody Up There Likes Me*, and I was fascinated with how he was, in a way, building on the fighter he had become for *The Battler*. We had a late dinner that night, and I asked Paul if he was consciously bonding the two roles.

"No, not that I expressly link them or even think that way, but certainly what residue there is from me as the battler seeps into me as Rocky. There sure as hell is no seepage from *The Silver Chalice*."

We both laughed.

"It's funny now," Paul said, "but after that debacle I really thought I'd never be in another movie, honestly. My confidence was shot and an actor without confidence is like a canoe up a creek without a paddle. I was grateful I was able to get that part on Broadway in *The Desperate Hours*. Tell you the truth, I thought that would be the only way for me—Broadway stuff."

"What was it about *The Silver Chalice* that was so terrible?"

"Everything. Every damn thing. It was a biblical costume epic in which I played a Greek slave named Basil and wore what looked like a cocktail gown that accented my skinny legs. I was paid a thousand dollars a week and it was the most painful money I ever earned. This sculptor had been commissioned to sculpt the face of Christ, who back in those Roman times was an unknown. Basil kept trying to envision this face and he kept working and working at it, and then all of a sudden, the bells went off, trumpets sounded, soaring violins and all that, and Basil sees a vision of Christ. In rehearsal the director said, 'So you see it, and then you go, Aha!' I said, 'Victor, if this guy really saw a vision of Christ, you'd think he would hallucinate, or faint, or do something like that. But to have this powerful vision and say, Oh boy, there's the new model of the Edsel and I'd better get to work on it . . .' That movie added luster and dimension to the word 'awful.' Virginia Mayo and Jack Palance were in it, and a couple of camels. I had to ride one of the camels. The gait of a camel is very uneven—just try to hit a camera mark on a camel. We were in terrible disarray. My first movie, and the review in *The New Yorker* was: 'As the Greek sculptor, Paul Newman, who resembles Marlon Brando, delivers his lines with the emotional fervor of a Putnam Division conductor announcing local stops.' Small wonder, when I had lines like: 'Helena, is it really you? What a joy!' Needless to say, I never got another call from Hollywood. And I wouldn't have gotten this call except for Jimmy's bad luck."

"Not really, Paul. Your performance as Ad Francis in *The Battler* is what did it. Jimmy's bad luck is what gave you the opening, but you made your own good luck."

"Yeah, well, maybe somebody up there really does like me."

MANY YEARS LATER, it was announced that *Silver Chalice* would be shown on television. Paul was horrified, having counted on this mummy not ever being disinterred. He said he was going to put a full-page ad in *The Hollywood Reporter* repudiating the film and requesting viewers not to waste their time watching it. Of course, the effect of the ad was to induce an unprecedented number of viewers to tune in.

Paul phoned me, deflated. "The ad didn't work."

"I didn't think it would."

"Why didn't you stop me?"

"I wanted to see it."

"So?"

"I didn't think your legs were *that* skinny."

*P*aul and I are fishing off the shore of Westport, Connecticut, where we both live, ten minutes from each other. *Somebody Up There Likes Me* was a very successful debut for Paul, and *The Long, Hot Summer* followed by *Cat on a Hot Tin Roof* were convincing proof that he was a spectacular newcomer to Hollywood's elite, earning him an Academy Award nomination. But this battered boat in which we are fishing belies his ascending-star status and that's just the way Paul wants it, stardom with no glitter.

The boat is an ancient wooden fishing boat with a small, abused outboard motor—four horsepower, if that—that clings perilously to its splintered stern. When we chug away from our slip at the Westport marina, put-putting past the opulent yachts and dual-rigged fishing sloops, we are subjected to finger-pointing and suppressed hilarity from the decks above us. "Hey, look, isn't that Paul Newman? What? In that . . . *thing*?" Tiller in hand, Paul grins and waves and enjoys the trek along the causeway as if he were a master yachtsman at the controls of a forty-two-foot Chris-Craft. Emblazoned on the crumbling bow of our boat is its name: *Caca de Toro*. On board are two paddles and a couple of rusty coffee cans: paddles for when the wheezy outboard poops out; cans for bailing the customary leakage. We are put-putting in this *Caca* because there is a five-year wait for a slip in the marina, and we had inherited the slip and the boat from someone who was moving away. I suggested replacing the wheezy

Fishing aboard Caca de Toro II *with young Timothy Hotchner.*

old-timer, but Paul said, "No, it's a classy antique. It's like we're in a remake of *The African Queen*."

This aversion to ostentation became a hallmark of how Paul dealt with the unyielding limelight that would be continuously focused on him. He gave no autographs. When I asked him why, he said the majesty of the act was offensive to him. Compliments also made him uncomfortable, "because I suspect they are just inane flattery. I much rather hear criticism because it's sincere." His closet contained one gray suit, a dark blazer, slacks, two neckties, and a couple of shirts. But when the *Caca's* outboard motor fell off its rotting perch and nose-dived to the bottom of the sound, Paul admitted it was time to upgrade and acquire *Caca II*, a secondhand Boston Whaler that the harbor master procured for us.

Paul and I both loved to fish but, sadly, we were the worst fishermen on the eastern seaboard. As anglers around us reeled in bluefish, stripers, flounder, weakfish, and blackfish, we watched with virginal envy, drowning our sorrows in Budweisers. That our bait disappeared, leaving our hooks empty, did not bother Paul. He loved the quiet and isolation of fishing. He would anchor at buoy 13, convinced, with no supporting evidence, that it was a lucky spot. We did catch a lot of worthless sea robins, hermit crabs, sand sharks, plenty of jellyfish, blowfish, and plastic containers, but nothing you could put in a frying pan.

We once went fishing in Key West with the famous guide Captain Sam. We spent an entire day at it, with Captain Sam switching baits and offering advice. "I been fishing these here waters nigh on fifty-three years," Captain Sam said, "and you two fellers are the first ones never even got a bite on your lines. Seem like the fish went outa their ways to avoid you."

CACA II SUFFERED a painful demise, battered to pieces against the dock by a sudden violent storm. Paul suggested that we go to the boat show at the New York Coliseum to find a replacement, but I was on my way to Hollywood to write and produce *The Snows of Kilimanjaro* for the *Buick Electra Playhouse*, so unfortunately Paul was left to handle the temptations of the boat show on his own.

On July Fourth, when we were in Westport at the same time, Paul enthusiastically met me at the marina for the presentation of *Caca III*.

"How do you like it?"

I was dumbfounded.

"Not another boat around here like it."

"I should hope not."

"Is that meant to be critical? I thought you got rid of your backwoods personality when you left St. Louis."

What confronted me was a two-story, square, floating object with a bright-yellow exterior, an inner staircase connecting the stories, a thick, nauseatingly green shag carpet on both levels, and a yellow-and-green striped canopy covering the entire upper deck with colored lights encrusted in the canopy. Instead of a horn, it emitted a musical blast that sounded like an armada of Good Humor wagons, and its hi-fi speakers could easily carry to New Hampshire. The boat would have been right at home in a Puerto Rican Day parade.

"It has a flat bottom," I observed.

"Of course. It's a lake boat."

"But this isn't a lake. This is part of the Atlantic Ocean and it has waves and things like that."

"Yeah, but don't worry, we can handle it."

Paul loved piloting the green-and-yellow monster along the coastline and into neighboring Southport Harbor, home of the ultraconservative Southport Yacht Club. Guiding the boat among the flotilla of opulent yachts, Paul delighted in gliding past the yacht club's veranda where members in their tartan blazers and orange pants were having their sundowners, often treating them to a *Caca III* salute on the super hi-fi or on the musical horn, sometimes on both.

The life span of *Caca III* was mercifully short. A sudden squall upended it, pitching us and our fishing paraphernalia into the turbulent waters. *Caca III* eventually washed ashore, a mangled green-and-yellow wreck. We had lost all our fishing gear, but it really didn't matter since we weren't catching anything anyway.

*P*aul is cooking lunch, his signature hamburgers browning over a white-hot charcoal fire, buns toasting, Budweisers and watermelon in an icy cooler, and a salad he is mixing with a dressing of his own concoction. Robert Redford and Jack Valenti, the Motion Picture Association president, are sipping beers and watching Paul adroitly toss his salad. Bob has a house ten minutes down the road, and Valenti is visiting from Hollywood.

"You grill a mean burger," Valenti says.

"Twenty percent fat," Paul says as he flips them over. "That's the trick. Only one flip. And no salt, salting them makes them tough."

"How can you have a tough burger?" Bob asks. "It's ground beef."

"Oh, I have," Valenti says.

"Redford, with your palate you could eat ground glass and not know the difference," Paul says, as he shovels the salad on plates and spatulas the burgers onto buns. We take Buds from the cooler and settle down around the redwood table beside the swimming pool.

"Bob, I hear you're doing Hotch's book, *King of the Hill*," Valenti says.

"Well, I'll be executive producer. I would have liked to direct it but the book was brought to me by a young guy whose first movie recently landed at Sundance, Steven Soderbergh. He knew that Hotch was a friend and asked me to help him get the rights. Of course, if you had sent me the book . . ."

"I didn't think it was your kind of subject—kids in the Depression," I said.

"Second time you let me down. Only part I ever wanted that I didn't get was in *Adventures of a Young Man*—young Hemingway disguised as Nick Adams."

"I tried but the producer, Jerry Wald, said you had no experience for a big part like that. I tried to get you a screen test but he refused."

"But Paul got a juicy part in it, didn't you?"

"I had done it on television," Paul said. "I made the mistake of repeating the way I played the battler on television. I should have reworked it for the film."

They were referring to a movie I had written that linked ten Hemingway short stories together, with one of the scenes featuring Paul in his role as the battler.

"The pity is," I said, "that Wald insisted on using Richard Beymer because he had him under contract for five hundred dollars a week. Richard came across as a willowy Hemingway, if that's the word. Thank God Ernest never saw it. He died four months before the picture was released."

"How you get experience without getting any experience beats me," Bob said. "I almost had the same fate as Sundance."

"Yeah," Paul said. "The studio wanted Steve McQueen, but Steve was being difficult about his billing—left of mine or an inch above mine or some such crap. And I had the same problem as Hotch—all you'd done was *Barefoot*. But when I offered to cut what they were paying me and my take of the gross, they caved in."

"I never knew that," Bob said.

"You owe me. Did you know, Jack, that up until the very last minute I thought I was playing Sundance. I had all the lines down and I started doing Sundance's lines, but George Roy Hill stops me. 'Wait a minute, Paul,' he says, 'you're not Sundance—you're Butch.' "

"How about you guys do a sequel to *Butch Cassidy*," Valenti said.

"Jack," Paul said patiently, "we got killed at the end."

"Not really. It's a freeze-frame of you shooting, but you don't outright die."

"There were a hundred soldiers firing their guns at us," Bob said.

"But you don't fall down and bleed or anything. Anyway, people don't remember details like if you really got killed."

"Jack," Paul said, veering away from his Butch reincarnation, "do you play tennis?"

"Oh, yeah. I belong to the Beverly Hills Tennis Club."

"Good. Tell you what, I know Redford's been hitting with a pro, how about doubles. Hotch and me, you and Bob. I've got rackets. Rules are a slug of beer every time we change sides and foot faults are okay up to two feet."

Paul carted the cooler of Buds out to the court, putting it in the lee of a net post. After a brief warm-up, we got under way. Bob was an athletic leftie with a good, solid stroke, but Jack was a short-legged five foot four at most, and saddled with an erratic forehand that often tended to catapult the ball over the fence or into the bottom of the net. Jack's partners at the Beverly Hills Tennis Club must have had infinite patience.

Paul was intense but inclined to swing too soon or too late. I had played tennis since I was twelve. From the outset it was apparent that Paul and Bob were treating this as a serious duel. We changed sides every odd game and paused to chug some beer.

As the match progressed, there were serious disputes over foot faults and line calls. To overcome Jack's erratic forehand, Bob induced him to lob every time he got the ball—the higher, the better. On the other hand, I instructed Paul to stay at the net where his quick reflexes earned points.

What also earned points for Paul was his superiority at drinking beer. Paul regularly consumed a dozen or so beers a day, and this intense training gave him a significant advantage over his opponents, who began to wobble under the sweltering sun. As a matter of fact, with every side-changing swallow Paul's game got sharper, and by the time the match ended in our favor, he was hitting respectable overheads and the rest of us were seeing two tennis balls in place of one.

That afternoon I came to realize how competitive Paul was. No matter what the challenge—mastering an impossible role, or driving a race car at two hundred miles per hour against experienced drivers half his age, or starting a business against daunting odds, or engaging in a public debate with Charlton Heston over nuclear power—Paul's competitive drive was an intrinsic virtue.

To overcome our reputation as the most inept fishermen on the East Coast, Paul and I planned several fishing trips that we hoped would establish us as certified anglers. But as fate would have it, all the trips had to be canceled for a variety of medical reasons.

Paul had heard about a fishing guide on Key Largo who was a specialist in bonefishing. The bonefish is a fierce fighting fish that inhabits shallow waters and is caught on a line that has to be adroitly cast in its path. To land it depends on the skill of the angler coordinated with the skill of the skiff minder, who uses a long pole to direct and propel the skiff in its silent journey; the bonefish are wary and avoid any disturbance, certainly the sound of an outboard motor.

On the day before our scheduled departure, Paul took his rod down to the bank of the Aspetuck River, which runs alongside his house, intent on practicing casting for the eagerly anticipated bonefishing expedition. That evening Paul called to say that he had had an unfortunate injury. On one of his practice casts he felt a snap in his elbow, followed by a blast of pain and a darkening patch on his arm. X-rays revealed he had ruptured a blood vessel in his casting arm, which was now in a sling.

Another time, a friend who had a deep-sea fishing rig invited us to come to Ft. Pierce to go after the big stuff. But we never got there. On the morning of our scheduled departure, when I went to brush my teeth I had such shooting pains in my hand that I couldn't hold the toothbrush. An emergency visit to my doctor revealed carpal tunnel syndrome. For six weeks I had to brush left-handed. I couldn't even shake hands, much less fish.

Late one spring we had planned to go to a Canadian encampment on the banks of the Salmon River to fish for chinook salmon at the peak of their run. We had outfitted ourselves with the warm clothing, waders, and other gear necessary for the four days we had planned on staying at the camp. Again, I was the one who caused the cancellation. Complaining of groin pain, I was diagnosed with a hernia that would require an operation as soon as possible.

And two days later, Paul found out he had a double hernia that put him in the hospital the same day I went in. Different hospital, same surgery. During the two weeks of convalescence, we phoned each other and compared conditions. We agreed that what we dreaded the most was sneezing, and trying to get out of bed in the morning.

*O*ver the years Paul could be counted on to support those he cared about. When I had a new play in tryout at a theater in St. Louis, Paul flew in to see the show and sat in the back of the theater, trying to be incognito. Paul trying to be incognito was like the figures on Mount Rushmore trying to go unnoticed. Afterward, we had dinner and he made some good suggestions about what I might want to consider on the rewrites.

Paul had a good friend, Ron Buck—an attorney who owned a Los Angeles restaurant with Paul as his silent partner. Ron nurtured a dream that some day a screenplay he had written would be produced. Paul had found out that Ron had cancer and decided to help him realize his dream. He worked on the screenplay of *Harry and Son* with Ron, but no studio would green-light it unless Paul would produce, direct, and star in it, with Joanne in a featured role. Paul and Ron continued to work on the script, but it defied significant improvement.

I visited the shoot in Ft. Lauderdale a couple of times (I had Newman's Own popcorn samples to evaluate), and found Ron in his glory. Paul even had a movie chair made with Ron's name on it, the kind of chair usually reserved for star performers. Paul paid a price, however, for this good deed because the movie, which never found its center, did poorly both at the box office and with the critics. But for

Paul it was a success because it fulfilled Ron's dream. Not long after the movie was released, Ron succumbed to cancer.

Paul often sent funds without being asked, and often anonymously, to actors he knew who were down on their luck, since he always tried to avoid what he called "noisy philanthropy." It seemed that Paul hurt for people who were hurting.

I was particularly touched by his support of Jim Padula, a shy, self-effacing man who for twenty years was a jack-of-all-trades for Paul and Joanne. After they acquired the eighteenth-century stone colonial across the stream from their original house on North Avenue, Jim replaced much of the outmoded plumbing and wiring. There was a large old neglected barn on the grounds that Jim converted into an imposing multipurpose house with an area for screening films. He re-did the interior with authentic oak beams and barn siding, and created a loft with guest quarters, which were reached by a spiral staircase. Paul installed a brass plaque on the barn: PADULA'S HOUSE.

In gratitude for all the things that Jim did to make their lives easier, Paul and Joanne sent him Christmas presents that ranged from a pool table to a Boston Whaler. Tragically, Jim became afflicted with stomach cancer that metastasized rapidly; he was only forty-two when he died.

During Jim's final weeks in nearby Norwalk Hospital, Paul visited every morning on his way to the Bronx, where he was making *Fort Apache the Bronx*. Every morning without fail. And many afternoons Joanne came to chat and do her knitting. On one of his last visits, Paul assured Jim, "Whatever your wife, Millicent, needs, we're there for her." Paul told me about the day Jim was working at the house and Joanne brought him a tray of Toll House cookies that she had just baked. In his shy way, Jim thanked her and said, "I wish there was something I could do in exchange for these wonderful cookies." Joanne said, "There is. You can teach me how to lay bricks." And he did.

. . .

I ACCOMPANIED PAUL on several of his daily commutes to the *Fort Apache* location, joining him when he visited Jim on the way in. Jim had done splendid work for me when I had bought my neglected house, which very much needed his expert restoration, and he was indeed a man of quality in his work and in his person. On those hospital visits we mostly talked about the movie, which had become an unexpected tribulation for Paul. He had been enthusiastic about the script and his role as Murphy, a hard-nosed cop who was trying to restore law and order to an area of the South Bronx that was riddled with poverty, crime, narcotics, and corruption. It was the kind of positive role with a social conscience that Paul felt would help him overcome his last two disasters, *Quintet* and *When Time Ran Out.* Paul also wanted this picture to do well since his new agent, the powerful no-holds-barred Michael Ovitz (Paul described him as a combination of a barracuda and Mother Teresa), had negotiated an unprecedented three-million-dollar fee for him.

Paul had worked hard to prepare himself for this role. Several weeks prior to the start of filming, he had spent time at the Forty-first Precinct, called Fort Apache by the cops who felt besieged by the ugly crimes surrounding them. Paul told me that his observation of life in the precinct station had provided him with the mannerisms and attitudes and speech of the cops—the way they carried themselves on their beat, how they made arrests and bookings.

This was the same method he had used to prepare for his role in *The Battler*, hanging out with the scarred professionals, especially the one who provided him with the substance of his character. There was a time later on when I asked Paul if discovering that early method had influenced his subsequent roles.

"Yeah, I learned from that *Battler* experience and used it in many other films. For *Somebody Up There Likes Me* I had the foundation of the battler, Ad Francis, to build on, plus I hung around Stillman's Gym in New York, the citadel for boxers, veterans, up-and-comers, and bums. I also spent time with Rocky Graziano, whose life I was portraying. The best part of acting for me, what I enjoy the most, is the preparation."

In a second memoir, *Somebody Down Here Likes Me, Too*, Graziano describes his encounter with Paul.

The studio arranges for me to meet Paul Newman and he shows up for the meeting wearin' beat up slacks and a T-shirt. We click it off right away, when he grins at me like he's known me all my life. "Whataya say, Rock!" he says. "I read your book, and I saw you fight. It's amazing to see you are a man of letters."

He makes everybody laugh, and even though he kids me I could see right off there ain't one thing phony about this guy. Maybe there was. He was too good looking. In fact, the guy is pretty. That didn't matter because I knew they could fix up an' flatten his nose for the part, an' if they couldn't I could do it for them. I could see in the guy's eyes that he was a fighter. He's got bright blue eyes, but when you look in 'em you see a hard look dancing around inside. Only one other guy I ever see these same eyes on an' that was another friend of mine, Frank Sinatra. When their blue eyes spot a wise guy, the eyes say, "Don't fuck with me, man!"

At that time, Newman was about twenty-nine or thirty, maybe three, four years younger than me, and his weight, around a hunnerd and sixty, was what I weighed during my best fighting days.

I find out the guy's an all-round athlete. Tennis, skis, swims like a fish, great ballplayer. The guy not only does 'em all, he does 'em good, and now I'm gonna teach him how to fight in the ring. When you see this guy with his clothes on, he's a fooler. I find out fast in the gym that Paul is a lot stronger than he looks.

I asked Paul about his character, Ben Quick, in *The Long, Hot Summer*, which also starred Joanne Woodward and Orson Welles.

"Well, I had to prepare myself for the dialect and attitude of a no-good smooth Louisianan who schemes himself into a highfalutin family. I went down to Baton Rouge a couple of weeks before production, and with the help of a newspaper guy, I was able to meet and hang out with a bunch of locals. There was one fellow in the group I focused on. He was huge, six-six or so, worked on an oil rig. I played pool with him—Brother Fochee was his name—and we drank a lot of beer. I got the gist of Ben Quick from the set way he carried himself. Confident. On top of his game. He walked into a room, took his position, and stayed put. Didn't move. He dominated everybody in the room. I folded some of that into Ben."

"And *Cool Hand Luke?*"

"Finding Luke took awhile. I went to Appalachia and hung out for a couple of weeks with tomato farmers. I fashioned Luke after a teamster I met down there in West Virginia. For the scene where I learn that my mother has died, and I play the banjo and sing 'Plastic Jesus,' I wanted to learn how to play it. I was told it was too difficult an instrument and that I would have to fake it. Well, I got someone to teach me and I played my own accompaniment in the film.

"For *Hombre*, where I played a white guy raised by Apaches, I went to an Indian reservation for five days and brought back one thing: I drove past a general store and there was a guy standing there in front with one foot up and his arms crossed. He was in the exact same position when I drove back four hours later. That whole character came out of that. I don't really have to get down on my hands and knees and look under the rocks. As a hot-shot pool player in *The Hustler*, I had to look the part at the pool table. The great champion Willie Mosconi was my teacher. I put a pool table in my dining room and Willie worked with me for two weeks before the flick started. He was a helluva patient teacher. And I had a good trombone teacher for *Paris Blues*—Murray McEachern, who had been in the Benny Goodman orchestra. I was an expatriate jazz trombonist and I got good enough to play on the soundtrack.

"For the Henry Gondorff character I played in *The Sting*, I watched many movies by a famous star of the thirties, William Powell.

I knew I couldn't come close to him but it would give me something to aim at. That was my idea of what I wanted to bring to that character.

"For *Road to Perdition*, where I played an Irish godfather, I sat down with Frank McCourt, who wrote *Angela's Ashes*, to tape his Irish brogue, not to imitate him but to give a faint flavor of that accent to my dialogue. That initial experience I'd had with that difficult character in *The Battler* became the modus operandi for many of the parts I played. But I always took my time to assimilate it. You don't attempt that kind of thing unless it finally becomes organic. Otherwise it's just an imitation."

I was privy to how Paul developed his hockey-playing manager in *Slap Shot*. There was an ice-skating rink in the neighboring town of Norwalk. Paul hooked up with a semipro team that played there, practiced with them, dressed with them, went to a local bar and grill with them. Paul also practiced every day on his own to build up his leg strength and improve his ability to handle his skates, the stick, and the puck. I went to a couple of the skirmishes and watched the team knock Paul around pretty good.

Paul had a good time making *Slap Shot*, which was shot in Johnstown, Pennsylvania. His favorite director and good friend George Roy Hill was in charge, and Paul was enchanted with the script, which was replete with raw dialogue and rough action. He gave me the script to read, and there was dialogue with words I had never heard in a film. Paul was delighted that it had been written by a woman, and that it was a down-and-dirty movie like no other he had ever been in. All the hockey players in the Johnstown arena were professionals, and although he had turned fifty, Paul was able to keep up with them.

When he returned to Westport after the film wrapped, he walked gingerly and ached all over, but he said he had never enjoyed making a film as much as that one.

. . .

FORT APACHE THE BRONX was not the positive experience Paul had anticipated. Playing a good cop in an embattled precinct in a dangerous, squalid neighborhood populated with thieves, junkies, prostitutes, pimps, and drug gangs, Paul was berated by a cadre of protesters who attacked the film because it made it appear that all Bronx citizens were as bad as the ones in this bad neighborhood. The protesters picketed the film's locations and shouted disruptive slogans when the cameras started to roll.

The *New York Post* played up the confrontation and described Paul as a false liberal who exploited the downtrodden citizens of the Bronx when his million-dollar paycheck was involved. The protesters formed a committee that demanded some changes in the script to depict the neighborhood in a more favorable light, but the producer and director refused to breach the integrity of the script.

After reading the diatribes in the *Post*, I called Paul to offer my sympathy for this unwarranted assault. "It's that son of a bitch right-winger Murdoch," he said. "He stirred them up because it's good copy, it sells papers. And, of course, I haven't got a way to fight back."

"Why not call a press conference? Meet them head-on," I suggested. "I'd like to come in with you tomorrow. Maybe some of the other papers will support you."

"Might help. I'll pick you up at seven. We'll stop at Norwalk Hospital on the way in and visit Jim."

Paul was very good at the press conference. He pointed out that in real life most of the criminals in the precinct jail were blacks and Puerto Ricans, and that was the reality of what was in the film—they were the criminals and that was a fact. Paul also pointed out that the picture depicted a couple of rogue cops who were white. "This picture will inform a wide audience of these terrible conditions in the Bronx," Paul said, "and that might bring about some positive improvements."

Paul's speech did no good. He was subjected to negative questions and denunciations.

At the end of that day's shoot, on our way back to Westport, I apologized for my suggestion. Paul waved it off. "I'm going to set my sights on Murdoch," he said, "and that awful gossip rag that grovels for him. But maybe I've got revenge here. I'm giving my part all I've got, and if the picture turns out okay, it will get an audience that will carry *my* message, not his."

Fort Apache did turn out well, but protesters, backed by Mayor Ed Koch, who said the movie "wasn't kosher," picketed the premiere in Manhattan. The reviews were uniformly favorable, and Paul received good notices. I congratulated him for being able to keep his acting steady despite the storm raging around him.

"I don't get seasick," he said.

Paul carried his grudge against Murdoch beyond the *Fort Apache* episode, often excoriating him in interviews, but Murdoch maintained the upper hand by sniping at Paul in the *Post*'s notorious Page Six, the conveyer of its low-down gossip. On one occasion, in connection with some contrived incident, Page Six listed Paul's height as five foot nine. Paul sent Murdoch a blistering challenge, suggesting a bet of a hundred thousand dollars if he was officially measured at five ten or more, designating me to hold the stakes. Of course, Murdoch weaseled out of it.

Paul also pursued other grudges, most of them political. He actively campaigned against Richard Nixon, whom he had deplored since Nixon's nefarious campaign against Helen Gahagan Douglas for a Senate seat from California. The photo that Nixon doctored to show Douglas with a Communist earned him the lasting sobriquet "Tricky Dick." When Paul was campaigning on weekends for the Democrats in the 1968 presidential election, he rented a Jaguar for the weekend. When he learned that Nixon was going to rent that same Jaguar during the next week, Paul left a note attached to the steering wheel: "This clutch is tricky, but you shouldn't have any trouble with it."

When Paul found out that he had been prominently listed on Nixon's enemies list, he called it the "highest single honor I've ever received."

Paul also campaigned against Ronald Reagan who, in his actory way, held views on environmental, social, educational, and wealth issues that were the opposite of Paul's. On the night that Reagan won the presidency, Paul invited a group of us to his barn where he screened *Bedtime for Bonzo*, in which Reagan's co-star was a chimp. On arrival we were provided with pots and pans to bang and rattle during the film. We had a raucous time of it, but after half an hour or so of watching the chimp make a monkey out of Reagan, we had exhausted our bedlam, abandoned our pots and pans, and trooped off to dinner.

Paul also had a fierce dislike of Charlton Heston, who had been a good friend and fellow Democrat during their involvement with the civil rights movement. But when Heston sacked his liberal principles and moved far to the right, Paul denounced him. One evening, Paul, Joanne, and I were watching the news when there was a report that showed Heston, a rifle aloft in his right hand, championing the sanctity of gun ownership before a cheering audience of the National Rifle Association. Paul snapped off the TV.

"He makes me sick," he said, "I mean actually turns my stomach."

When Heston began making television appearances on behalf of Reagan's Star Wars defense program, Paul appeared on programs condemning it. This led to a vitriolic televised debate between the two of them. Years later, when he found out that Heston was scheduled to introduce him at a ceremony inaugurating the Scott Newman Foundation, Paul had him uninvited and replaced by Donald Sutherland, who shared Paul's enlightened beliefs.

*W*e are in the *Caca de Toro* at buoy 13 eating meatball subs from Fortuna's, washed down with Budweisers, fishing lines with non-bobbing bobbers in the water. Paul is between movies and is restless. His last two films, box-office disappointments, have rankled him. "They were not fun, just jobs. It's time to get out of the acting racket."

"And into what?"

"Joanne and I ate at a pricey restaurant last night with bad service and bad food. How about we open a restaurant?"

"Us?"

"Yep."

"Here in Westport, the graveyard of restaurants?"

"Yep."

Paul fancied himself as a limited but accomplished chef. His repertoire was centered largely around hamburger, steak, scrod, salads, and a chicken soup that he concocted from broth from the health-food store, chicken from Boston Market, mixed vegetables from Stop & Shop, and various seasonings.

"You got a place in mind?"

"No, but I have a name for it—Newman's Own. It would be a red-blooded American restaurant: great hamburgers—through the grinder twice—fresh corn on the cob, potato skins, an imaginative salad bar with my salad dressing, knockout desserts, and vintage wines.

Our specialty would be our signature ten-dollar hamburger with a hundred-dollar bottle of Château Lafite."

"And what are the two of us going to do in this Newman's Own restaurant?"

"I'd tend bar and you'd be the Ingratiating Greeter."

"So you think people are going to flock to this restaurant in order to pony up to the bar where this famous movie star is mixing drinks, snapping close-ups with their instamatics, making small talk with the superstar, that's how you think it will go?"

"Nice proposition, isn't it?"

"Well, how about this proposition. In comes a party of six Wall Street guys and their wives, all permed and perfumed for the occasion. After a couple of rounds of martinis, the six Wall Street guys go to the Ingratiating Greeter and say, 'Where is the superstar bartender we have come all the way from Greenwich to clink a glass with?' 'Oh,' says the Ingratiating Greeter, 'at the moment he's on the beach in Miami sunning himself in between takes on the movie that's shooting there. Sorry, but maybe he'll be in next time.' At which point the six Wall Streeters, who have come all the way from Greenwich with their permed and perfumed wives, kick the shit out of the Ingratiating Greeter."

"With your mastery of judo, you'd be able to handle them."

Over the following weeks, Paul led me around to a series of places where we could raise the Newman's Own banner on our restaurant. There was an Italian restaurant, Il Villano, that had just closed its doors; a Chinese restaurant located on the second floor of a building on Carriage Hill that was closing down; a furniture store in a landmark building on the Saugatuck River that was in the process of being converted into a hotel with a contemplated restaurant on the top floor overlooking the river. We looked at these and many more, but Paul found defects in all of them—not enough parking space, not big enough to turn a profit, not attractive. None of them measured up to his phantom requirement that it have an all-American appeal, whatever that meant. When Paul departed to make a film on the West Coast, I thought I had heard the last of his restaurant enthusiasm, but on his return he continued to look at expiring restaurants in Westport and neighboring towns. Paul's restaurant fantasy ended one day, however, when we ran into a friend of his who had recently closed down his restaurant and told us why: "We were always filled and we had people on the waiting list, but the restaurant never turned a profit. I was skimmed up front and bled out the back—bartenders skimming cash as it passed from bar patrons to the cash register, waiters skimming in cahoots with the bartender, kitchen help ferrying food under their coats as they went out the rear door. That and a dozen other scams and suddenly I'm not paying my bills. Maybe you guys have a solution for all that."

After that encounter, Paul never mentioned the restaurant project again. Many years later, however, Paul did get his restaurant, but it was not called Newman's Own and it was not devoted to an all-American, corn-on-the-cob cuisine. It was called the Dressing Room, and his partner was Michel Nischan, a celebrated chef who featured many of his signature dishes on the menu. Paul built the restaurant next to the Westport Country Playhouse, which he and Joanne restored to its glory days. To his consternation, clips from his movies played endlessly at the bar, but he did succeed in getting a pretty good hamburger on the menu.

*P*aul is on the phone. "My friend Jonathan Demme called to invite me to a screening of his new film. Want to go?"

"Sure."

We take a cab to the address Paul has written on a scrap of paper. Eleventh Avenue, far downtown in a dangerous-looking neighborhood.

"Doesn't look right, does it?"

The usual screening rooms in Manhattan are in midtown along Fifth Avenue and Broadway. We get out of the cab and reconnoiter. A couple of porno shops, a dimly lighted bar, a storefront with heavy curtains and no name, a tattoo parlor, a bodega. We go to the door that bears the address we were given. Inside is a dark, forbidding lobby with a creaky elevator that, clanking slowly, takes us up to the floor number on Paul's paper. Sitting on a deck chair, facing the elevator, is a woman with a clipboard. She gets up to greet Paul. She is very tall and tries to smile. "Greetings, Mr. Newman," she says, ignoring me. "We're ready for you." She unlocks a door and leads us into a large, deserted screening room.

"Are we early?" Paul asks.

"No, sir. Please settle in, and when you are ready just press the button on this remote." She hands the remote to Paul, walks to the door, and leaves. I distinctly hear the door being locked.

Paul shrugs and selects a leather chair at the back of the room. I sit about ten rows from the screen.

"What are we seeing?"

"Beats me."

"Didn't Demme tell you?"

"Nope."

"Pretty weird, huh?"

"Yep."

"Why did she lock the door?"

"Beats me."

"Me, too."

Paul hits the button, the room goes black, and the movie begins: *The Silence of the Lambs.*

As the movie gets further and further into Hannibal Lecter's evilness, I get further and further spooked by being a prisoner in a locked room in the neighborhood from hell.

Suddenly, at the scariest of Lecter's blood-curdling behavior, a voice booms, "Hotchner!"

I levitate.

It was Paul.

"You want me to come down there and hold your hand?"

*P*aul called to announce that a sleek, high-powered Chris-Craft cruiser had just arrived in our slip and that he would meet me at the marina in forty-three minutes to take it out on its maiden run. Paul always set his rendezvous time in precise minutes, invariably hitting his mark. *Caca IV* was indeed a fine-looking twenty-one-foot speedboat with an inboard motor, a 99 percent upgrade from *Caca III*. I asked Paul if the boat fairy had put it under his pillow, but no, he had been given the boat from Chris-Craft as a reward for posing beside it for a publicity photo.

As soon as we hit the open water, Paul shifted *Caca IV* into full throttle, its nose springing perpendicularly, a heavy spray churning over us, the torque pinning me against my seat back, Paul whooping it up as the boat knifed through the yielding swells.

Paul had doted on speed ever since his portrayal of an Indy 500 driver in the movie *Winning*. Back then, he had owned a big Harley and enjoyed zooming along the streets and back roads of Connecticut, enjoyed, that is, until one fateful afternoon when rounding a sharp curve at high speed he hit gravel and skidded violently, the impact pitching him over the handlebars and into the ground face-first. The impact would have probably destroyed his face, but a split second before impact, he managed to thrust his hands forward; the gravel tore all the flesh from his hands. A few days later he showed me his hands, which were peeled raw. He sold the Harley

and never rode a motorcycle again. Nevertheless, he retained a zestful enthusiasm for the bicycle, which he demonstrated remarkably as Butch Cassidy. He made light of his near catastrophe on the motorcycle: "I missed a great opportunity to remake myself as Boris Karloff," he said.

Paul also wanted speed in his off-track automobiles. For years he drove a Volkswagen outfitted with a Porsche engine and disc brakes. Many's the time he would stop to pay a toll on I-95, with a customized high-wheeled hotdogger in the adjoining toll bay—young bucks looking down derisively on the movie star at the wheel of the puny Volkswagen. Paul relished these moments when he'd let the hotshots zoom away from the toll booth with a commanding lead, only to see the little Volkswagen go sailing past them, the movie-star driver with his middle finger aloft.

After the Volkswagen wore out its welcome, Paul supercharged a Volvo with all the racing paraphernalia it could bear. On one occasion, while we were tooling down two-lane Route 77 in the Volvo at a fairly good clip, Paul was pulled over by an unmarked police car. The trooper said, "Did you know you were going eighty-five in a fifty-five zone?"

"It was an illusion, Officer," Paul said. "I was just testing a car at the Lime Rock track going a hundred and forty—so going eighty-five was like going fifty," at which point he gave the officer his driver's license. The trooper took one look in the car and exclaimed, "Oh, God, if I give you a ticket my wife will give me hell for a week." He returned the driver's license. "That Sundance movie, you sure did good," he said as he returned to his unmarked car.

We were now in the Volvo going at a good clip along the Merritt Parkway en route to a lunch meeting in Boston, Paul extolling the outstanding virtues of the Volvo as it accelerated into the passing lane, whizzing past several cars as if they were stationary, when the Volvo's engine suddenly coughed, sputtered, and exploded with a plume of smoke as it expired. Paul kept it rolling onto the shoulder. He raised the hood and allowed all the smoke to escape. He stood looking at the smoldering engine as cars zoomed by.

"Do you have Triple A's number?" I asked.

"Hotch," Paul said patiently, "Triple A cannot touch this car. There's only one man who knows how to handle it."

"Where's he?"

"New Jersey."

"You're driving a car that can only be serviced by a guy in New Jersey?"

"So what? New Jersey is the next state."

"New York is the next state."

"Well it's the Garden State Parkway, just over the Tappan Zee Bridge—let's see if I can reach him."

"That's four hours away!"

"Three."

Paul dialed the car phone (this was before the cell-phone era) and fortunately made contact. "He's on his way."

"Does he have a key?"

"Why would he need a key?"

"To get in the car."

"Why would that be?"

"We're going to lock it, aren't we?"

"You think we're going to go off and leave my Volvo here *unattended*?"

"We're not?"

Paul phoned and canceled our lunch appointment.

I took stock of our waiting area. There was a guardrail behind us with thick vegetation and trees beyond it. It was a warm spring day. I went over and sat on the guardrail. Paul took a box from the glove compartment of the Volvo and came over to the guardrail to join me.

"Lunch," he said, jiggling several jelly beans from the box into my hand.

"Licorice. Good. One of my favorites," I said with mock enthusiasm.

We sat on the guardrail and munched on our jelly beans. Passing cars slowed down at the sight of the disabled Volvo and the two stranded motorists on the guardrail. Paul began explaining his theories on what had caused the eruption in the Volvo's engine. He really had schooled himself very well on the functions and dynamics of the sophisticated engine and suspension of a racing car; the engine under the hood of the Volvo was a far cry from a traditional Volvo engine and obviously its sophistication is what had caused the trouble.

Sitting there on the guardrail in the bright spring sun, only a few feet from the passing cars, Paul was being recognized by passing motorists who were startled to see this stranded superstar. Slowing, they'd roll down their windows and call to him, and now cars began to pull onto the shoulder and offer assistance. The stopped cars attracted other cars to stop, causing a slow-down on the parkway. Paul sensed that there could be trouble. He stood up and called out, "I don't need help. Thanks, but please get back in your cars." At that time Paul was the country's number-one movie star, and this opportunity to meet him was not lost on the motorists. Imagine being able to tell your friends that you had *the* Paul Newman in your car.

Paul swung his legs over the guardrail and disappeared into the thick vegetation. It was a perfect maneuver. With their quarry gone, the motorists reluctantly returned to their cars.

When they had left, Paul came back, and until the tow truck with the New Jersey guru arrived, we sat on the guardrail facing the vegetation, our backs to the traffic.

I HAD FOLLOWED Paul's entry and gradual progress in the specialized world of racing from the very beginning. To prepare himself for his role in *Winning*, Paul enrolled in Bob Bondurant's School of High Performance Driving. When he first drove a beginner's Datsun on the track, Paul told me he felt a surge and an adrenaline rush like he had never felt before. Within no time, he was pushing a Lola T270 over 150 miles an hour. For the Indy 500 sequences of *Winning*, Paul had advanced to the point where he could do his own driving in an open-wheel car against professional drivers in a race staged for the cameras. *Winning* did not do very well at the box office, but Paul always felt indebted to the film for having set him on the racing path.

By now, Paul had acquired a six-seater jet with two full-time pilots, which enabled him to move easily from one track to another. I accompanied him to many of these meets. In the beginning, when he was just testing cars and familiarizing himself with the various tracks, I also flirted with the possibility of learning to race, but when, after a few introductory lessons and Paul's encouragement, I made an attempt to maneuver the track at Lime Rock at a modest one hundred miles per hour, I knew I would never have the skill or the guts to deal with the speed.

But that's what Paul thrived on—the challenge of pushing himself to go faster, especially around the curves and doglegs and other challenges of the track. In some of his early races he was too slow in the trials to qualify for the event, but he was never disheartened. "I've got to go at it my way," he once told me. "You've seen how I am getting into a part. It takes me quite awhile. I've got to take my time and let it settle in and give it its head until it becomes organic, a part of me. That's how I am with these cars. I'll get there, but it won't be fast."

Once Paul found his level, he went all out. "I was never much good at any sports—football, skiing, baseball, tennis—name it, I was mediocre if that. But when I get behind the wheel now, I know I've finally found a sport I'm good at." He entered a lot of races at Lime Rock, a Connecticut park a few hours from Westport, where I sometimes watched him compete. Slowly he was moving up in line in his finishing positions.

He was also building a solid rapport with his crew, who are as vital to the driver as a *quadrilla* is to a matador. Paul talked shop with his crew, cooked burgers for them, swapped ribald jokes, and enjoyed their company more than being with the "in" people on the coasts.

The crew related to him as a driver, not as a movie star. When he was with them the talk was about differentials and spoilers and torque and transmissions, not about billing and grosses and close-ups—and Paul loved it.

Finally, in 1976 all of Paul's long preparation paid off. Just as Butch and Luke and Hud finally emerged, so did P. L. Newman, the racer. He had been competing unsuccessfully for several years at Road Atlanta, where the national title competition of the Sports Car Club of America was held. Now, finally, driving a Triumph TR6, he won the national championship. It was glorious to be the national champion racer in his class. I called to congratulate him. "It's like getting four Oscars with wheels," he said. From that moment on, professional racers accepted him as one of their own.

Over the years I was often at the track to witness his triumphs and his occasional catastrophes. I was at Lime Rock in the viewing stand, along with Joanne and two of their children, when Paul was in a ribbon race that had attracted several top drivers. There was also one qualified woman driver, a rarity on the circuit. Paul had qualified toward the head of the pack of twenty-eight cars. His expectations were high. His car was in great shape. He had just won the past eight events on the Sports Car Circuit and a second national championship in Atlanta. Winning the Lime Rock event would give him the points he needed to lead his field.

At Lime Rock the race starts on a straightaway but then quickly encounters a dogleg. The racers followed the lead car once around the track, then at the flag there was an instant acceleration for position on the turn. All of our field glasses were zeroed in on Paul. We saw him cut off two front-runners on the turn, then revving up on the straightaway he started to pull out front when a car to his rear rammed into him, knocking him off the track, careening him across the adjacent field and out of the race. Elapsed time: twenty-six seconds and no points. The driver who had hit him also spun out of the race. It was the woman driver who climbed out of the wreckage.

Paul had always praised the gods for his good luck, and there were several instances when he needed their blessings. I attended one race at Lime Rock when Paul's brakes gave out and he hurtled into the trees going 150 miles an hour. To avoid a head-on collision, Paul maneuvered his car so that the opposite side scraped along a stand of trees, the sliding impact slowing down the car and bringing it to a smoking halt. It was a very skillful maneuver and more than likely saved his life.

At another track, Paul was sideswiped, causing his car to roll over and catch on fire. Trapped in his seat, the flames advancing in back of him, he kicked out the windshield and escaped before the car went up in flames.

There were a few races when, as a result of spinning out and hitting walls, he nursed sore ribs and bruised knees—and a bruised ego—but he never broke a bone, suffered a concussion, or landed in a hospital bed.

In 1975, when Paul was making *The Drowning Pool* in New Orleans, he took a day off from filming to run a Porsche with a passenger on a nearby track, a risk not usually permitted during filming. With the Porsche running flat out at 130 miles an hour, Paul crashed spectacularly. Again, an anticipated dire outcome from the look of the wreck, but Paul and his passenger emerged relatively unscathed. In the track's interview room Paul described what had occurred: "Neither of us had a seat belt, and for a time we rode on two wheels, then the car went on its side but we weren't thrown out. The windshield shattered. Fortunately it was European glass that breaks into powder on impact. We climbed out of the window. Neither of us was hurt. We hardly had our hair mussed. As I stood by the car, somebody slammed the door on my hand. Fortunately the door was sprung or I would have lost the tips of my fingers. 'Open the door,' I said quietly. When they did I ran to the beer cooler and stuck my fingers in the icy water. I didn't even lose my fingernails."

In 2000, when he was seventy-five and competing at the Daytona International Speedway, he crashed going 185 miles an hour, but only suffered some damaged ribs. When we had lunch several weeks later, he got up from the table gingerly. "Ah, Hotch," he said, "I used to be a fast number, but now the ribs won't let me forget them."

But the persistent rib pain did not deter him from getting behind the wheel. Two years later I went with him to a race at Watkins Glen, New York. Going over one hundred miles an hour, he had a bad spinout and crashed. From the looks of the wreckage, I feared Lady Luck had deserted him. But the track crew pulled him out and, although limping, he walked away from the tangled mess with only a few bruises.

He once took me on a couple of victory laps after a big win at Lime Rock. He had lapped the field, going 148 miles an hour on this challenging track with its abrupt doglegs and irregular elevations. Now I was placed against the metal rigging and told to hold on tight. When you watch a car negotiating a track at 140 miles an hour on the straightaways, you do not relate to the speed, but when you are inside that car, it is an entirely different perspective. Which is to say: I was scared shitless. Paul went into sharp curves at speeds I was sure he couldn't navigate. When we hit the elevations the tires left the roadway. At the end of the ride, the crew chief had to help me pry my fingers loose from the roll bar.

Of all his many victories on the track, none pleased him more than being on the team that won the twenty-four-hour Daytona race. But coming in second in the Le Mans twenty-four-hour race in southern France, driving all night in a pelting rain, the speedometer around 200 miles an hour, rated a close second.

None of Paul's zest for racing was shared by Joanne—she had played Paul's unfaithful wife in *Winning*—and from the outset she tried to discourage his infatuation with the challenge of going faster and faster. When she, in the midst of filming, learned that Paul had gone to the Indianapolis 500 track and was clocked driving a lap at 143 miles an hour, she let him know how she felt: "Paul, I'm too young to be a widow." Actually, racing aside, their marriage was very solid. In 1958 they had performed together with good chemistry in *The Long,*

Hot Summer. A year later they got married in Las Vegas and honeymooned in London. But their honeymoon was cut short when Paul had to leave for Hollywood to start work on *Cat on a Hot Tin Roof* with Elizabeth Taylor.

As for the racing, I was often at meets when Joanne was there to show her support. But she was always fearful and unhappy watching Paul drive in a phalanx of aggressive cars only a few feet apart, her husband jockeying at 150 miles an hour with drivers half his age. But as the years passed and Paul proved his mettle, he worked out an agreement with Joanne: he would go to the ballet and opera with her in exchange for Joanne tolerating his racing.

I CELEBRATED MANY of their anniversaries with them. On their first anniversary, they invited my wife and me to have champagne with them at their rented apartment on Fifty-first Street in Manhattan, then go across the street to what Paul described as a little French restaurant that they had "discovered." The little French restaurant turned out to be Lutèce, the reigning four-star restaurant at the time.

On their twenty-fifth anniversary, they repeated their marriage vows before a gathering of family and a few friends at their Westport home. Joanne wore a gorgeous antique gown of white lace that I'm pretty sure she did not wear at their Las Vegas wedding. Their five daughters also wore white and their dear friend Stewart Stern, who wrote several of their screenplays, officiated with a masterfully written discourse about love and the beauty of shared lives. Paul asked me to photograph the proceedings, which I did with my new Minolta. Alas, when I developed the film it was blank. I had not known that my fancy new camera required a special battery for the lens. Luckily someone else had a camera and pictures do exist, but for years Paul would rib me about my invisible photography.

Nell, Susan, Stephanie, Lissie, and Clea rather glumly celebrating Paul and Joanne's twenty-five years of wedded harmony.

*P*aul had a selective memory. Although he was an encyclopedia of telephone numbers—just give him a name and he'd give you the number—he struggled to identify faces. I can't tell you the number of times he'd say to me, sotto voce, "Who is that?" We were once on a flight from Los Angeles to New York when, as we entered the first-class cabin, he spotted a face. "Hotch, quick, who is that? I just finished a flick with him." "Paul Sorvino," I whispered. "Hiya Paul!" he said on the way to his seat.

We were having lunch in New York at Madame Romaine de Lyon's omelet shop, when, on the way out, Paul passed a table where an attractive black woman was sitting. She greeted him, and he said, "I just sent you a check." "You did?" the woman said, obviously surprised but delighted. "Well, thank you very much." Paul stopped me outside the restaurant. "Who was that?" he asked. "Diana Ross," I said. "Good God!" Paul returned to her table. "I'm sorry, Diana," he said, "it was Jessye Norman I sent the check to. You singers mix me up. But if you've got a charity, I'll be glad to send it something, too."

Paul's forgetfulness caused him to leave belongings everywhere he went. Sunglasses, briefcases, scripts, clothing, car keys, directions (he sometimes had to turn his car around and go back for them), and he regularly forgot to put cash in his pocket, relying, to paraphrase Tennessee Williams, on the kindness of fans.

But occasionally Paul's forgetfulness worked to our advantage.

When we were raising awareness for a children's camp we were sponsoring in Ireland, Paul went on the BBC to elicit contributors.

He received an inquiry from the trustee of an organization called The Duke's Trust. Writing on behalf of the Duke of Manchester, Paul Vaughn explained that the Duke desired to meet and discuss the possibility of sponsoring, on behalf of the Trust, a camp like ours in the U.K.

Vaughn identified the Dukes of the Trust as:

The Duke of Norfolk, KG, CB, CBE, MC.
Earl Marshal and Hereditary Marshal and
Chief Butler of England; Premier Duke and Earl.

The Duke of St. Albans
Hereditary Grand Falconer of England;
Hereditary Registrar, Court of Chancery.

The Duke of Argyll,
Chief of Clan Campbell;
Hereditary Master of the Royal Household, Scotland.
Admiral of the Western Coast and Isles.
Keeper of the Great Seal of Scotland.

The Duke of Manchester,
Viscount Mandeville.
Baron Mantagu of Kimbolton.

The Duke of Wellington, MVO, OBE, MC.
Prince of Waterloo (Netherlands).
Marquess of Torres Vedras and
Duke of Vitoria (Portugal).
Duke of Ciudad Rodrigo.

Paul and I had lunch with the Duke and Duchess in London that summer to explore the possibility of a camp outside London.

The Duke, an affable, natty, loquacious, distinguished gentleman, explained that such a camp would be in the purview of the Trust, and he proposed that we advance to him, on behalf of the Trust, the sum of $200,000 as seed money for the camp. With that many dukes behind it, Paul felt it had a very good chance of coming to fruition, and since it was his policy to invest each country's profits in their charities, he decided to use the U.K. profits for the payment to The Duke's Trust.

When Paul got into this with the Duke, he joked about the possibility of getting our own dukedom—a Duchy-on-the-Thames—or at least getting tapped on our shoulders by the queen and made honorary knights. Sir Paul, Sir Hotch—not a bad ring to it. Rubbing elbows with duchesses and earls.

Paul signed the relevant documents, and we went back to London for the express purpose of meeting with the Duke of Manchester and giving him the proposed $200,000. But that's when Paul's forgetfulness saved the day. When he reached in his pocket for the check, it wasn't there. He had left it in his hotel room. Paul apologized and set up a meeting for the following afternoon.

The next day we had lunch with John, a London friend of Paul's, before going to meet the Duke and Duchess to deliver the $200,000 check, which Paul now did have in his pocket. In the course of that lunch, Paul mentioned that we were funding the Duke of Manchester for the purpose of starting a camp in England.

A look of immense incredulity flooded John's face. "The Duke . . . of *Manchester!*"

"Yes."

"Two . . . hundred . . . thousand . . . dollars!"

"That's right."

A wave of laughter rose from John's belly, an unrestrained full-throttled guffaw, his face reddening as he choked on his laughter, tears coursing down his cheeks. "Two . . . thou . . . the Duke . . ." He coughed laughter into his handkerchief. "No you're not," he finally managed to say, as he dried his cheeks and blew his nose.

"Not what?"

"Forking over two hundred thou U.S. to the Dupe of Manchester."

"You say 'Dupe'?"

"My dear fellow, you may be awed by this duke business, but get this picture—bloke on the docket at the Old Bailey on criminal charges that he and some confederates tried to obtain thirty-eight thousand pounds from the National Westminster Bank in Streatham, down south from here, and what do they post as security for the cash? American bonds that are counterfeit. So while this bloke is in criminal court, he gets word that his brother or uncle or some such has kicked off and this indicted criminal, this black sheep of the family, is now the Duke of Manchester. All over the papers."

"This is my duke?"

"Your very duke. His barristers somehow maneuvered to get him acquitted, but I had a helluva laugh over what the judge said at the end of the trial: 'On a business scale of one to ten, the Duke is one or less—and even that flatters him.' "

Paul had located the missing check that had mysteriously appeared at the bottom of his shaving kit, but he was not about to hand over $200,000 to a duke who was rated one or less. Instead he hired a snoop, one of those Fleet Street ferrets who sniff out the dark and scurrilous items that they then feed to London's hungry tabloids. The snoop discovered that The Duke's Trust existed in name only, and that the Duke's ancestral seat at Kimbolton had been sold, which meant that the Duke of Manchester had no property, in fact was the only duke listed who had no territory. Needless to say, the $200,000 transfer did not take place, and although constantly pursued by the duke and his cohorts, who exuded an overwhelming passion for helping sick children, Paul avoided any further contact.

But the snoop, true to his calling, continued to send bulletins about the Duke. In 1996 came snoop word that the Duke had once again been hauled into court, this time in Florida, where he was accused, along with four others, of defrauding the Tampa Bay

Lightning ice-hockey team. The Duke had been made honorary chairman of the team in 1991, on the basis of promising to raise $25 million for them in bank loans. The money was supposed to come from a Dublin company, Link International, whose chairman was the Duke, with a fee of $2.5 million being paid to the Duke and Link. But shortly after the Tampa Bay Lightning had advanced $50,000 in fees, Link went out of business. At the trial, the Duke's lawyer said his client was "more of a dupe than a duke," that the Duke was the perfect fall guy, and that every time he was involved in the transactions, someone was handing him a drink. "He was used," his lawyer pleaded, "because he's gullible, he's vain, he's foolish, but none of that is a crime." The Duke did not take the witness stand and was straight-out convicted on four counts of fraud. He served twenty-eight months in the state penitentiary, where he ran the laundry. He died in August 2002 under mysterious circumstances. And with that bulletin, the snoop signed off.

*O*n the morning of November 21, 1978, I sat down to breakfast, opened *The New York Times*, and recoiled at this terrible headline:

PAUL NEWMAN'S SON, 28, DIES OF A DRUG OVERDOSE

It was reported that Newman's son, Scott, had died in a Los Angeles hotel room of an accidental overdose of alcohol and tranquilizers. According to the article, Scott had been staying at the Ramada Inn in West Los Angeles for several days.

Scott had been taking pain pills for injuries sustained in a motorcycle accident, and the police presumption was that the pain pills combined with his intake of alcohol caused his death. An official finding would be entered after a pending autopsy.

The article described Scott as an actor, stuntman, and nightclub singer who performed as William Scott and that his mother was Paul Newman's first wife, Jackie Witte, who was divorced from him in 1956. The article went on to say that Newman had been notified at Kenyon College where he was directing a school play.

I FIRST MET SCOTT when he was visiting his father in Westport. He was around twelve or thirteen. Paul lived in a big house on North

Avenue then, and when I arrived, Scott was performing nimbly on a large trampoline that was rigged up on the commodious lawn. Scott soared to an impressive height and executed graceful somersaults and twists. I introduced myself and complimented him on his athleticism. He was a handsome boy, big for his age, with a ready smile and an easygoing personality. He said that some day he hoped to do "the real stuff on the high trapeze with Ringling Brothers."

Scott lived with Paul's first wife in Los Angeles, but he was at one prep school or another most of the time. When Paul, who had been stoking his charcoal grill, came over to join us, Scott seemed to quiet down and become somewhat deferential. Paul said some good things about Scott's work on the trampoline, but they didn't seem comfortable with each other.

I didn't see Scott again until he was in his late teens. He was six feet tall, taller and more muscular than Paul. Scott had had a very rocky teenage passage, getting dismissed from one prep school after another for "detrimental behavior," which included insubordination, inattention to his studies, and use of drugs and alcohol. Paul had ascended to the heights of superstardom, and being his son was proving more than Scott could handle. Scott was handsome but not his father's classic handsome.

I didn't see much of Paul during this period. He was letting his extreme popularity get in the way, letting his stardom exploit him. He was drinking too much and participating in a freewheeling life without boundaries. I was in Hollywood when he was co-starring with Steve McQueen in *The Towering Inferno*, a disaster movie about a fire in a high-rise building. I visited Paul on the set and found him sitting alone, outside the camera area, dressed in torn, smoke-stained clothes. He was subdued, his natural energy diluted.

"First time I fell for the goddamn numbers," he muttered. "I did this turkey for a million and 10 percent of the gross, but it's the first and last time, I swear, you heard it Hotch, last time ever for the big contract. Every day here is like going to the dentist. You want to know what chicken shit goes on? McQueen actually made a count of our lines of dialogue and when he found out I had twenty lines more than he did, he made the producer fatten up his part so he had the same number as me." Paul's "towering" take turned out to be $12 million but it didn't mollify his feelings about the film.

We had dinner that evening at Romanoff's, a celebrity restaurant in Beverly Hills run by a phony prince. Paul had several drinks before he looked at the menu. He had just triumphed in *The Sting*, which had been an enjoyable romp, thereby rendering the *Towering Inferno* experience doubly painful. But on this occasion he was brooding about Scott, not the misery of the part he was playing.

"I guess you read about Scott's dustup with the cops? The papers were full of it."

"Yes," I said. "Poor Scott."

"Poor Scott, my ass, kicking a cop in the head!"

Scott was now twenty-three years old. He had dropped out of Washington College after two years to work small movie assignments, mostly stunts on Paul's films, beginning with *Sometimes a Great Notion*. He had started skydiving when he was in college and afterward made five hundred parachute jumps in order to get certified as an instructor, but he left when he was not put on staff. He bummed around after that, working in construction, driving a ski-resort bus, waiting tables, all the while refusing to ask his father for money or for any real help in getting him acting lessons.

Paul did help him in other ways. George Roy Hill was directing *The Great Waldo Pepper* (Paul had turned down the lead, which went to Robert Redford), and at Paul's request Scott was given a small part in the movie but George refused Scott's entreaty to let him do stunts on the wings of the biplane used in the film. But Scott got into trouble before he reached the film's Texas location. Staying overnight in Bridgeport, California, Scott had a lot to drink at a local bar and when the barman shut him down, Scott staggered off belligerently and slashed the tires of a school bus that was parked down the street while boisterously singing the Washington College anthem. Sheriff's deputies soon appeared and Scott vehemently resisted their attempts to arrest him, trying to fight them off before they succeeded in handcuffing him and getting him into the backseat of the squad car. While en route to the police station, Scott was able to raise his legs and kick the driver in the back of the head with his heavy boot, causing the car to skid off the road. He continued his truculence in the police station and was charged not only for the misdemeanors of public drunkenness and the damage to the school bus but also with the felony of kicking the police officer with his boot, which legally was considered a dangerous weapon.

"I got him a really good lawyer," Paul said, "and when his case came up yesterday the judge dropped the felony charge, only convicted him of a misdemeanor and put him on probation for two years. I paid the thousand-dollar fine. Of course, the papers made a big deal out of the arrest but nothing about it being just a mis-demeanor. The friggin' *New York Post* put the story on the front page. 'Paul Newman's Son Kicks a Cop in the Head.' "

"He's frustrated, Paul. He wants to be an actor, follow in your footsteps, and he wants you to be proud of him."

"Yeah, I know. I was that way. I wanted my father to be proud of me, but he died before I got it going. That's a big regret—that he never got to see that I did amount to something."

"Did it occur to you that Scott getting drunk and vandalizing the bus is like Cool Hand Luke getting drunk and vandalizing all those parking meters? He so wants to be like you."

"I want to straighten him out but, speaking of Luke, I guess you'd say that 'what we've got here is a failure to communicate.' I'd like to talk things out with him but, as you know, I'm not much of a talker. When we do get together, we talk about sports and other stuff. We avoid the trouble spots. I've got a shrink lined up for him and I've got him set up with a good acting program. Maybe the shrink can get to where I should go. It doesn't help that Scott doesn't visit us anymore. He doesn't seem to have any friends. I should see him more, I guess, but with the movies and all . . ."

Over the course of the following months, Scott tried to clean up his act. He stopped drinking and using drugs, and he joined a health club and exercised regularly. Paul called me one day to tell me that Scott was going to appear on *The Merv Griffin Show* that evening. Scott handled himself very well. He was spontaneous and likable, and radiated good humor. I called Paul to tell him how impressed I was with how he had handled himself. He said he had just talked to Scott, congratulated him for his performance, said he told Scott he wanted to help him in any way he could.

Not long after his appearance on *The Merv Griffin Show*, Scott was cast in a guest role on a top-rated TV series, *Marcus Welby, M.D.* Paul invited a dozen of us to come for dinner and watch the show. I don't recall the details of Scott's role, which was largely confined to a hospital room where he was a patient. Paul watched him intently, commented favorably during the commercials, and at the end, when Scott's name appeared on the crawl, he phoned Scott in Hollywood and complimented him. I thought that Scott had performed capably but without any charisma that would distinguish him from run-of-the-mill television actors. Although we never discussed it, I could tell that Paul knew in his heart that Scott was not destined to have a career as an actor.

In the months that followed, Scott did manage to land two or three parts on TV series, but after a while the assignments petered out and so did Scott's belief that he could make it as an actor. But he still wanted somehow, some way to prove himself, and he decided to try to establish himself as a cabaret singer, appearing in small clubs as William Scott. I was in Los Angeles when he was appearing at a night spot on Melrose Avenue. He was drinking at the bar when I arrived and we greeted each other with a warm hug. He performed a set of three songs with the club's three-piece combo. He sang pleasantly, presented himself in an attractive way, not trying to do too much, styling himself after Frank Sinatra's easygoing manner. But the room was not responding, treating him as a background to the hubbub of their conversations.

Afterward, Scott and I had a few drinks at the bar. He wanted to talk about his father, who hadn't spoken to him for several months. Scott hoped his cabaret act would lead to an album, "something Pop can be proud of." I asked him why he didn't call Paul. "No," he said, "I don't want him to think I want something from him, like money. I don't want him to think I can't support myself."

"Can you?" I asked.

"No. I borrow from my friends."

"And when that runs out?"

"That won't happen," he said, heatedly. "I'll always manage. I can do stunts."

"Aren't you still mending from that motorcycle spill?"

"Yeah. I had to quit the health club. It's my ribs. But I'm mending. Booze helps and a couple of lines now and then." He sipped his drink. "It's hell being his son, you know. They expect you to be like him, or they try to get to him through me. All of fucking Hollywood seems to have screenplays they want me to give to him. Or for him to show up somewhere or another. I'm Paul Newman Jr., you know what I mean? But I don't have his blue eyes. I don't have his talent. I don't have his luck. I don't have anything . . . that's me. What do they want of me, Hotch? What do *I* want of me? All I have is the goddamn name."

That's the last time I saw Scott. The album never happened. There were no more cabaret bookings. Scott was back on a regimen of alcohol and drugs. He had no money and often cadged lodging with friends, sleeping on a couch or a makeshift bed on the floor. Paul and Joanne, aware of his plight but finding it difficult to breach his defenses, did manage to provide psychiatric help, which Scott accepted. Dr. Mark Weinstein was the psychiatrist who was looking after him, making himself or one of his associates available to Scott at all times. On the day of his death, one of Scott's friends gave him a bottle of Valium, most of which he swallowed immediately. Feeling panicked, he called Dr. Weinstein, who sent a member of his staff, Scott Steinberg, to bring Scott a prescription of Darvon and to stay overnight with him in his rooms at the Ramada Inn. For several weeks

Dr. Weinstein had been concerned about Scott and had often arranged for one of his associates to keep an eye on him.

On the evening of his death, Scott had decided to retire early. He went into the bedroom and took some quaaludes along with a line of cocaine. Several hours later, Steinberg became aware that Scott was struggling to breathe. He immediately called 911, but Scott had lapsed into a coma and the paramedics' efforts to revive him failed, as did the emergency procedure at the hospital. Scott's death was recorded on the morning of November 20, 1978.

I debated whether to call Paul. What was there to say? I knew he was at his alma mater, Kenyon College, directing students in a play. I decided I had to call him. After I asked for him, I waited a long time for him to come to the phone.

"Hotchnik," he said. His voice was thick and hoarse.

"I just want you to know I'm here for you," I said.

There was an interminable pause. Paul was by nature a slow responder, but this was different; he was dealing with an emotion he probably had never felt before.

Finally, he said, "It's a hurt beyond tears."

He and Joanne flew to the West Coast and, after a brief private service, attended to Scott's cremation. On the flight to Kenyon, Paul considered withdrawing from his commitment to the students, but by the time he arrived back on campus, he had decided that he needed to honor the commitment, that he needed the distraction of the theater, that there was plenty of time to grieve and to deal with his guilt, which would stay with him for the rest of his life.

It wasn't until much later, when we were in the Bahamas scouting locations for a movie, that he finally talked about Scott.

*P*aul adored classical music and he had a sound system that certainly delivered it with the highest fidelity. When we had lengthy sessions in his study, he often filled the room with an unusual Bach transcription or his favorite Bernstein Mahler. As his hearing slowly degenerated (I think it was exacerbated by the deafening roar of the race cars), the volume of his music increased to compensate; there were times when we were forced to shout over the music, but Paul acted as if turning down the volume of a classical recording was a form of disapproval.

One afternoon we were lunching on his housekeeper, Caroline's, exemplary chicken salad and Paul was being effusive about the previous evening when he and Joanne had gone to the Glimmerglass Opera in Cooperstown, New York, and heard a renowned countertenor who had the most rapturous voice Paul had ever heard.

"Have you ever heard a really great countertenor?" he asked.

"No, I don't think so."

"You're in for a treat."

Interrupting his chicken salad, Paul put on a CD of the countertenor, the hi-fi brilliant, the volume high, Paul rhapsodic.

To tell the truth, I have a zero record with countertenors. As a matter of fact, I prefer a good soprano in the high registers. For a few minutes I did rather enjoy listening as Paul's countertenor reached the operatic stratosphere that defies ordinary tenors, but this was a long-playing CD and I can assure you that a little countertenoring goes a long, long way. But Paul enjoyed every minute of it and seemed to heave a regretful sigh when the countertenor mercifully delivered his farewell aria.

More to my liking was Paul's infatuation with chamber music. To celebrate his eightieth birthday, Paul invited thirty of us to a small venue in Westport where he had arranged for the renowned Emerson String Quartet to play a program of his favorite pieces. Following the recital, the audience and the artists were invited to a catered dinner at Paul's converted barn.

It was a glorious program of music. It is one thing to hear this world-famous group playing from the stage of Lincoln Center's Avery Fisher Hall and quite another to have them performing in such an intimate setting.

I phoned Paul the following day and told him how much my wife, Virginia, and I had enjoyed the extraordinary evening of music.

"Well, it's nice you enjoyed it," Paul said, "but that's the last time you're going to hear them."

"Why? Are they breaking up?"

"No," Paul said, "I just got their bill."

At long last, the intrepid anglers conquered the bone fish.

*P*aul and I are having dinner at P. J. Clarke's, a onetime speakeasy that still looks like a speakeasy with its old battle-scarred tables, checkered tablecloths, and menu written in chalk on a giant slate board at one end of the restaurant. Paul is drinking Michelob and I am drinking a Beefeater gin and tonic. When Paul suggested this dinner I could tell that he had something special on his mind.

He was studying the menu board. "What's it going to be?"

"I don't know. You know the basics here."

"Yeah. I'm partial to their grilled chicken breast."

"I think I'll do the salmon."

"Done."

He was sitting with his back to the restaurant, as usual, to keep from being recognized. Most of the time it didn't work, but Clarke's old-time waiters with their long aprons and quick feet were very good at keeping interlopers at bay.

"You heard about the First Artists thing I'm in on?"

"Well, what I've read in the papers."

"My agent, Freddie Fields, put it together. Streisand, Poitier, and me at first; now there's Dustin and McQueen. You know the drill? We choose the films we want to make, our company produces them, we get no salary but a percentage of the gross. In this way, we run our own show with no interference from the majors."

This wasn't the first time movie stars had formed their own company. Back in the twenties and thirties, when I was a teenager, the reigning superstars—Charlie Chaplin, Douglas Fairbanks, Mary Pickford, and the director D. W. Griffith—had formed United Artists under similar auspices. After much initial hoopla, the arrangement lost its impetus when the stars made very few films for their company, and those films were inferior; they continued to do their better, successful films for the same studios as before. I remember expecting that they would all be in films together, but it never happened.

"It's not going very well," Paul was saying. "None of us has produced a hit. My two were thudders—*Pocket Money* and *Judge Roy Bean*. Lee Marvin and I just didn't get *Pocket* going, and although I had a good time with John Huston and the *Judge*, I guess the audiences didn't. Barbra and Dustin have made a couple of blockbusters but not for First Artists."

Paul signaled the waiter for another round. Two giggling women with cameras dangling from their necks approached the table, but a waiter adroitly intercepted them. "I want to give First Artists a good piece of work," Paul said. "I want to give *myself* a good piece of work. It's about time." He drank some of his fresh beer. "I've been thinking about that Hemingway story you once described back when we were doing *Adventures of a Young Man*."

I tried to recall what Hemingway story I had mentioned to Paul. " 'After the Storm'?"

"I read it and think it would be a good bet for me if you can pull it off like you did *The Battler*—how many pages was that?"

"Ten."

"What about it?"

" 'After the Storm' is only six."

"So you'll only have to expand it for a hundred pages or so," Paul said, laughing.

"Hemingway was around to fill me in on *The Battler*. He's long gone now."

"But now you've got me—I'm full of good ideas. Okay?"

I drained my gin and tonic. "Okay," I said, not at all sure I could pull this off.

Our waiter came to the table. "I think I'll change my mind and have the hamburger," Paul said, "medium rare and suffocated with onions."

"AFTER THE STORM" is a six-page soliloquy, delivered by an unidentified beachcomber, about a dramatic event that befell him in the Bahamas. With a fierce storm raging, the beachcomber has a fight in a barroom, knifes his assailant, and to avoid capture is forced to flee into the harrowing storm.

He manages to locate his boat and ride into the churning sea. Next morning, all is calm but wreckage is everywhere. The beachcomber discovers a lagoon where a large luxury yacht has capsized, entombing all aboard. The beachcomber dives to the wreckage, which is laden with jewels and gold, but try as he might, he cannot break into the boat. In the end he has to abandon it.

At its heart, the story touches something common to everyone: the desire for a windfall against great odds—finding sunken treasure, multimillion-dollar lottery payoffs, television quiz-show bonanzas, long shots at the racetrack, a twenty-dollar flea market painting that turns out to be a Cézanne.

To achieve a viable screenplay I would have to provide Hemingway's spare story with characters and action that would stay true to the basic story while injecting valid conflict and resolution. And to do that, I had to answer a number of questions.

Who is the man telling the story? An American? A limey? A wanted fugitive? Who was the man he fought with? An old enemy? What would have happened if he had succeeded in entering the wreck? What would he have found? The story mentions a safe with gold in it. If he had found it, how would he have opened it and what would he have done with the contents? Did he have a woman in his life? Two women? If he did collect the booty from the wreck, would there be someone who would try to muscle in on it? Would he be apprehended for knifing the man he fought with? Would he escape with the loot or wind up empty-handed as he does in the Hemingway story? Above all, the character at the heart of the action would have to be a challenge for Paul to portray.

I expected it to be tough going, but the screenplay virtually wrote itself—knowing Hemingway as well as I did and knowing Paul even better certainly helped.

I had expected Paul to like the screenplay since his character and the action had his kind of humor, invention, surprise, and perversity, and I was right.

"Since it's all in the Bahamas," he said, "let's go down and scout the three P's—places, people, and permissions. I've never been to the Bahamas. We should have some fun with this."

I had been to Bimini with Ernest the time he participated in an international fishing tournament, but I hadn't been to any of the scores of outlying cays where much of the action in *After the Storm* would take place.

I soon received an itinerary for our Bahaman adventure. The National Airlines flight from LaGuardia was met on the Ft. Lauderdale tarmac by a Cessna 310 that took us to Bimini. We checked into the Bimini Big Game Fishing Club in Alice Town, a village in north Bimini that attracted sports fishermen from all over the world for the big game fish that cruised its waters.

Two government dignitaries were on hand to welcome Paul and present us with a "Bimini libation." They started to give Paul a schedule for the following day, the highlight of which was lunch with Bimini's governor and other "important persons," but Paul had wandered out on the club's deck where he was admiring the fleet of deep-sea fishing boats in the harbor. He thanked the dignitaries for their invitation but said he planned to hire a rig the next morning and go after one of the big marlins or swords.

That evening I suggested we go to the Compleat Angler Hotel

BRISTED-MANNING ⚑ TRAVEL SERVICE
INCORPORATED
509 Madison Avenue, New York, N. Y. 10022

PLaza 2-8320   •   Cables: Brimatravl

Itinerary for Mr. A. E. Hotchner and Mr. P.L. Newman   10/10

Sunday Oct. 14   Check in with National Airlnes, LaGuardia Airport.
                    Duty Supervisor: Miss Cecilia Kumar.
                    You will have the V.I.P. lounge prior to departure.

                    LaGuardia - Ft. Lauderdale NAL 19   12:55 PM
                                                            3:28 PM

                    Tilford Flying Service: Tel.305 683 4121

                    Pilot Richard Coller will meet you at Ft. Lauderdale
                    Airport. At disposal Cessna 310 # 4069 Q. Depart for
                    Bimini Island.

                    Bimini Big Game Fishing Club. Sent cable advising
                    arrival.Advise pilot to radio ahead. Tel.No.Bimini 13.

Mon   15   Visit island and depart for Marsh Harbor, Abaco Island.

                    Suggestion : Guana Harbour Club,Great Guana Cay,
                                 This is near to Man O War Cay, which
                                 you approach by boat. Pilot can advise.

Tue   16   Abaco

Wed   17   Fly to Harbor Island, the norbern airport for the
                    island of Eleuthera.

                    Suggestion: Roberts Harbor Club , Spanish Wells
                                The owners/managers are good friends of
                                Stu Hall, the chap you talked with in NY.

                    Charter price includes leaving you at Harbor Island
                    and the dead head cost back to W. Palm Beach. If
                    you keep the pilot and plane this will be another
                    $100 (to the 18th October).

Thu   18   Eleuthera

Fri   19   Eleuthera . Reservations confirmed for the Cotton
                    Bay Club at Rock Sound. Managers are Franz and
                    Christine Gross. Pay bill directly.

Sat   20   Fly Rock Sound to Kennedy PAN AMERICAN 206 1:15 PM
                                                                  5:15 PM
                    (flight stops at Nassau but no change of plane)

Reconfirm return flight with Pan Am at Rock Sound by the 17th if possible and give Cotton Bay for contact.

Take proof of identification. No health shots required.

for dinner. It was where Ernest stayed the many times he fished Bimini and he had mentioned it in his writings. I had dined there with him and recalled that it had an unusual menu and an ambience that I thought we could use in the film. The proprietor, Helen Duncombe, gave us a tour of the old hotel and showed us memorabilia from the days during Prohibition when rumrunners made the Compleat Angler their headquarters, sometimes gunning each other down in disputes over prized routes and customers. The wine list was exceptional and so was the variety of fish that was presented to us on a silver tray. Paul was particularly taken with the conch salad, which contained green peppers, bird peppers, onions, and fresh lime. We agreed that the barroom and other features of the hotel would be ideal for certain scenes. Helen Duncombe said she would be more than happy to cooperate.

Early the following morning Paul clobbered my door and announced breakfast on the deck in five minutes. The sun was just rising but he was all set for our deep-sea adventure: long-sleeved shirt, a long-billed Bimini cap he had purchased in the equipment shop, tennis shoes, and his customary out-size sunglasses. He had chartered a handsome thirty-foot fishing rig manned by a grizzled captain named Mordecai and his equally grizzled mate named Trinity. As we left the harbor, Mordecai gave us a jar of pomade to rub on our exposed areas. "Put it on liberal," he said, "or the sun'll cook you like a grouper floppin' in a skillet."

It was a long run out to the prime fishing waters. Paul stood in the bow and got a kick out of the curtains of flying fish that peeled away from the advancing boat and the schools of dolphin that ran alongside. Captain Mordecai served coffee as thick as crankcase oil and Trinity passed hot buttered biscuits. "Hotchnik! Let's dump our Westport joints and live down here," Paul shouted over the engine's throb. "Yeah," I said. "We could open a fish store and call it Newman's Own. I could pipe the customers aboard and you could fillet the fish." Paul threw his biscuit at me.

Mordecai quieted the engine and Trinity took two large fish out of the ice chest. He attached them to the arching riggers and lowered them into the water. The fish being used for bait were bigger than anything I had ever seen anyone catch. The boat began to troll now, its engine reduced to a purr. Paul kept his eyes on the riggers. The captain went up to a topside control where he had a better view of the water. The sun had now found us full force. I put on more pomade and tossed the jar to Paul, who slathered it on his face and the back of his neck. Trinity offered us cheese sandwiches but we passed on them.

"How's it look, Mordecai?" Paul shouted.

"Always look like nothin' till there's somethin'," Mordecai said.

Paul gave me a look and went over to a side banquette. "Hey, Trinity," he said, "got a beer?"

"Sure do. All you want." He brought us a couple of beers with a name I had never heard of.

"You ever go back empty-handed?" Paul asked.

"Try not to," the captain said.

Paul realized now that the captain was not a conversationalist, so he laid back on the banquette and chugged his beer.

When it hit it was not just a tug on the line, it was a furious assault on the rig, the line screeching out, the whole boat rocking from the action.

Trinity grabbed the big fishing pole and harness. "Okay, Mr. Paul!" he called. "Come and get set." As Paul hurried into the fishing chair and donned the harness, Captain Mordecai was steering the boat in a circle to cut off the fish's escape path. Paul took the pole from Trinity, set his feet in the stirrups, and pulled back on the severely bent rod.

"Holy shit," he said, "this is a locomotive."

"You've got yourself a tussle," Trinity said.

The captain was maneuvering the boat in an attempt to bring the monster fish closer, but it was keeping its distance. Paul was straining against the harness as the line gave no slack.

"Give him a little line," Trinity said.

The unwinding reel sang a high-pitched squeal until Paul put on the brakes. Mordecai called down to Trinity. "Give him gloves!"

I looked at Paul's hands—they were already getting raw and blistered. He put on the gloves that Trinity gave him. "I'm going across the line," Mordecai called. "When I tell you, try to reel in." The boat made a tight turn. "Reel in!"

With great effort Paul was able to force the reel a couple of turns. Sweat was running down his face and his shirt was soaked.

I figured at least twenty minutes had passed.

"You've got a big daddy," Trinity said. "Don't want to leave home."

The line slacked for an instant and Paul reeled in but then the fish attacked in a new fury and Trinity had to keep Paul from getting pulled out of his chair.

"I can spell you for a bit," I said.

"No," Paul said, "it's my fight."

Mordecai called to him. "Mr. Paul, our line is snagged on the side of the boat. This'll take a lot of doing. I think we better cut it loose."

"Hell no! I'm gonna get the sonofabitch!"

"I can't guarantee—"

"Don't cut him loose!"

Watching Paul hold his position as the marlin delivered one ferocious charge after another, I thought of Cool Hand Luke taking punch after punch but getting back up on his feet, refusing to give in. I wanted to go behind his chair and help keep it from jerking forward, but Paul had made it clear that this was his fight.

As the battle continued, Paul began to yell at the fish, letting it know who was winning, calling it names, shoring up his will to keep his hands from giving up. They were painfully frozen around the rod, perhaps cramping, but Paul was not to be denied. This is how he wins races, I thought. And beyond races—this is his mind-set. One hundred fifty pounds of him against a ton of fish, and he's positive he's going to win.

"Okay, line's freed up," the captain shouted. "I'm gonna run him behind the boat."

The line pulled taut as the boat swerved, but then as the captain straightened out and made a run, the line began to ease, and Paul wheeled in the reel, the line slowly giving way until it slumped and Paul brought in the huge, beat black marlin beside the boat.

Mordecai came down from the bridge and helped Trinity rope the surrendered fish and secure it to the side of the boat. Mordecai radioed ahead and when we arrived at the Bimini dock there was a crew waiting to raise the marlin with a winch and tackle. Roped by its tail, they raised the giant fish up on the scale to be weighed, hanging upside down. As a tribute to its noble fight, Paul had the crew tie his own feet together and hang him upside down beside his defeated antagonist.

The following morning, although seriously stiff from his marlin tussle, Paul got himself aboard the motor launch he had chartered to scout the outlying cays that were on our list as possible locations for the film. These small islands, only accessible by boat, had indigenous populations, some of them dating as far back as the 1600s—independent, religious people who maintained their isolation by fishing and by farming their land. That these cays, some only forty-five miles from the Florida coast, were so untouched by tourism and modern development could be attributed to the Gulf Stream, which formed a barrier between Florida and the Bahamas. The stream was so brutally turbulent and had wrecked so many boats over the years that not many yachtsmen would brave it. Until recently the Bahamas had been a British protectorate, and the accents and mores we were to encounter reflected that. Paul was so enchanted with the places and the people and their way of life that at virtually every stop he announced that he was going to renounce Westport and move here.

OUR ODYSSEY BEGAN with Spanish Wells, a beautiful, tidy island with majestic coconut palms and a panorama of red-roofed yellow houses surrounded by luxuriant vegetation. Some of its 850 residents were descended from 1648 seafarers whose ship was wrecked on the treacherous reefs surrounding the half-mile-wide cay. And there were other Wellsians who traced their lineage to Loyalists, who in 1783 renounced the revolutionary new government of the American colonies and migrated to Spanish Wells. The British accents and customs had been retained over the years and, as a result, Paul and I felt that we had gone through a time warp and been deposited in an eighteenth-century fishing village. All along the coastline, the Spanish Wells fishermen, in their signature broad-brimmed hats, were trimming their nets and working on their boats. "I swear," Paul said, "I think we've wound up in the middle of a musical being shot on a 1933 MGM back lot. The costumes, those pretty boats, the neat little houses, all that netting strung out like that—any minute now they'll probably break into a jolly sea chantey led by Bing Crosby."

That afternoon, while being escorted by a local guide, we came upon a cricket match in full swing. Paul was fascinated by the performance of the batsman. "I don't know a thing about cricket," Paul said to our guide, "but hitting that ball doesn't seem too difficult."

"It has more spin and movement than you'd think," the guide said. "Would you like a try at it?"

"No, I don't want to disturb their game."

"Quite all right, they don't keep score anyway."

Paul put on batter's pads and stepped up to the wicket. After a few unproductive swings and misses, he began to regularly strike the ball. Although he was a dud hitting a golf ball or a tennis ball, and he had not been able to make the baseball team in school, Paul had finally found his calling. The Wellsians applauded as he finished his stint at the wicket. "There's no cricket in Westport," he said, "so I guess I'll have to move to England."

That evening, the Spanish Wells Cricket Club invited us to their banquet. They served a sublime grouper, one of Paul's favorite fish, and presented him with a cricket cap. He was invited to play the next afternoon but Paul said that, regretfully, we had to move on. In the morning when he came to breakfast, Paul was wearing his cap—said he had slept with it next to his pillow.

ON GREAT GUANA CAY, a picturesque little isle—very high elevation, abounding with coconut palms—we stayed at the charming Guana Harbour Club where we had vintage rooms overlooking the harbor. In contrast to Spanish Wells, the predominant accent here was Cockney, which the Guanans said originated in the nineteenth century. Cockney sailors on British vessels that passed through had jumped ship for the pretty Guanan girls and the inviting Guanan lifestyle.

The day we arrived was the annual Guy Fawkes gala that attracted boats from all over the Bahamas. A wild boar that had been caught in the surrounding woods was turning slowly on a spit in the barbecue pit. It was served that evening along with other local treats, while fireworks penetrated the sky and poor Guy got his annual immolation. Paul thought that the beach and vegetation where the fireworks took place was just right for the beach home of the character he would be playing in the film. Musicians from the boats— playing fiddles, accordions, horns, and drums—got together and improvised music that set the crowd dancing. Even Paul, who didn't like to dance, danced with his cricket cap on the back of his head.

Hours later, when I got back to the Guana Harbour Club, I found Paul having a nightcap beer in the bar. A jolly woman with a flower in her hair was playing nimbly on a piano that had two teeth missing.

"You've lost your cricket cap."

"Yeah. While we were dancing that circle thing with our arms in the air, my cap fell off and a pretty young thing with red hair ran off with it."

"Doesn't matter. I don't see you sporting it when we get back."

"Some of these Cockneys are so Cockney I can't understand them, but have you ever had so much fun? And did you notice? Not one autograph seeker. Now that's politesse."

"Paul, they don't have movies or television. You don't exist here."

"Wonderful. I'm going to buy a house on Spanish Wells and join the cricket team."

THERE WAS ONE cay that we ruled out despite our anticipation that it would be uniquely qualified for an important scene. Only four hundred people lived on Mores Island but outsiders didn't know much about them. Nor had anyone visited the island for years. But a couple of old-timers told us there were strange caves on the island where pirates had once stashed their loot, caves that no one entered because they were believed to be haunted. It was also believed that the four hundred islanders were descended from pirates who eventually settled there after the British navy put them out of business.

The driver of our motor launch had difficulty locating the obscured stone steps that led up to the level of the island. It was a steep climb, some of the steps covered with vegetation. At the top there was a clearing that contained a huge cross made of stone and a wood shelter with two entrances marked M and F. "Good," Paul said as he headed for the M entrance.

The shelter had no roof but the walls were sturdy and there was a flagstone floor. On the wall opposite the entrance there were two urinals attached to the wall. They were standard-size urinals at a not-so-standard height—approximately the height of our chests.

We stopped in our tracks, shocked.

"Holy shit!" Paul said.

We stared at the urinals, then we gave each other a look.

"Let's get our butts out of here," Paul whispered.

And we did.

In a hurry.

THE NEXT CAY we visited, Man-O-War, a concise, hilly island only two and a half miles from end to end, completed the Bahaman polyglot. Most of Man-O-War's population was descended from a group of two thousand Irishmen who settled there after being excommunicated from New York in 1783. These descendants had propagated the thick Irish brogue of their ancestors, some of them with dark skin and red hair to go with their brogue. So within a few miles of each other there was American English, British English, Cockney, and Irish brogue.

Man-O-War was busy with the commerce of precision boatbuilding, farming, and fishing, and we found several ideal locations, including the cemetery where all of the deceased were buried facing the sea.

An unexpected find was the sail-making business of Norman Albury. Norman and his wife, Lena, had been making sails for half a century. The old foot-pedal sewing machines and handmade tools were still serviceable, and the Alburys' attractive daughter was producing custom-made hand-sewn canvas jackets that bore the Norman Albury logo. Paul and I ordered a couple of these. I still wear mine all these years later, but, as usual, Paul forgot his somewhere a week after we returned.

In the time we spent on Man-O-War, we got to know Norman quite well. He told us about his father and grandfather who were sailmakers before him, turning out sails for the old schooners and fishing boats used during Prohibition by rumrunners who attempted nocturnal landings on the Florida shore.

"But now," Norman told us, "my four sons have no interest in continuing Albury Sailmakers. They're into boatbuilding and farming and such. I'm fine with that. We talked it out and agreed they should do what's good for them. A young man has to go his own way or his future turns on him."

When we left Norman's shop, Paul was in a contemplative mood. He took a path that went down to the beach and sat on the pink sand under a copse of palm trees.

"I'll be at the Dock 'n' Dine Docktel," I said, sensing he wanted to be alone.

"No, wait—I'll go with you a little later."

I found a shaded spot with my back against one of the palms. We sat for awhile, then Paul said, "Norman knows how to be a father. The way he is with his four sons. And I only had one."

Paul picked up a handful of the fine, pink sand and let it run through his fingers. He did it again and again.

"I could have talked to Scott, you know. I meant to. I tried to. I'd invite him for dinner and that afternoon I'd rehearse in my head what I was going to . . . things to ask him, things that might get him talking to me. Scott pushed me away, you know. He was so damned resentful that he was Paul Newman's son. Anyway, I'd get all rehearsed and we'd talk but I never got around to the things I'd rehearsed. Instead, I'd talk about my racing or my race team or about Scott's skydiving or his work at the Naval Academy—nothing that touched on any of his problems. I knew he drank too much and drugged himself but I didn't know how to open a door into him. He'd get kicked out of school and I'd talk to the headmaster so I knew the problems but . . . I knew the problems and I wanted to call Scott and sit him down to talk but . . . Christ, all I did was use my influence to get him accepted by another school."

Paul closed his eyes and leaned his head on his arms.

"I was the same with my father," he said in a muffled voice. "That distance. I wanted . . . I wanted to feel we were together. That he liked me. That I was his *son*. The closest we ever got was when he shook my hand. I don't think I ever hugged Scott or patted him on his arm or back or rump—the things fathers do. I never talked to him about his being an actor—can you imagine? He didn't have the talent—I should have been realistic with him. There are other things he could do besides jumping out of airplanes. But what did I do? I tried to help him get more acting jobs, which did nothing but make him more aware of his failures and more into booze and drugs to cover up his inadequacies. My own father died before I got going as an actor, so he died thinking I was a failure. That still bothers me . . . a lot."

Paul laid back on the sand and looked up at the sky between the palm fronds.

"Scott died before he had a fair chance to be a success . . . at something," he said to the sky. "I think about him . . . often . . . it hurts. The guilt. The guilt. All I could have done . . . and didn't do."

I said, "You did what you could."

"We know a lot of fathers, don't we, Hotch? How many of them have had kids who gave up and committed . . . and died? Oh hell, why don't I say it—committed suicide. That's what Scott was doing—slowly committing suicide. And I was watching it happen. And all I did was make more movies and be a big star."

"Paul, listen to me. I've been around from the beginning. I've watched you with Scott and I've been alone with him and listened to what he had to say. He had the resentment that a boy has when his father divorces and leaves him fatherless—in Scott's case, leaves him in a house with his mother and two sisters, three females who pretty much ignored him. Unlike most boys, Scott had a father who everyone knew—intimately you might say—who was on the big screen at the neighborhood cinemas, was all over the magazines, the newspapers, television. He was being a father to his new children in his new home. He simply didn't have the time to manage more than one family along with his big-time career."

"Hotch, you're as good a friend as I've got. I had to let all of this out of me or I'd explode. There's nothing you can say that will repair my guilt about Scott. It will be with me as long as I live."

"You're being much too hard on yourself."

"No, I'm not being hard enough. How do you make amends for something you can't make amends for?"

He got up and dusted off. There was a half-moon in the pale Bahaman sky. "Let's go to the Dock 'n' Dine," he said.

OUR FINAL STOP was Rock Sound, where a small airport on the far side of the cay serviced Pan Am's two daily flights. We were booked into the fashionable Cotton Bay Club, a special dinner had been arranged to welcome Paul. His honeymoon with anonymity had obviously come to an end, and the autograph seekers and camera buffs were back. They were civilized intruders, however, compared to the many uncivilized episodes I had witnessed. A battalion of paparazzi lying in wait outside a premiere, restaurant, hotel, or theater create a frightening melee when they go into action. On some of these occasions I had been battered away by the paparazzi in their frenzied attempts to get their lenses as close to Paul as possible. I was with him at the Watkins Glen track when, finishing a beer outside his trailer, he tossed the can into a refuse basket. A crowd of spectators had been gawking at the trailer and now some of them made a beeline for that coveted beer can. Pitched battle erupted at the refuse basket, pushing, punching, yelling, pandemonium, a beer-can scrum. On another occasion I had seen a similar eruption over a half-eaten apple that Paul left on a table outside his trailer at Lime Rock.

The manager of the Cotton Bay Club said that they were planning to serve suckling pig at the dinner, which would be attended by the governor and other officials and such notables as Juan Trippe, the head of Pan Am, who had a house nearby. The manager said they were going to hunt for the pig in a dense copse of brambles and trees at the far end of Rock Sound. These wild pigs had been set loose years back when a freighter carrying them and other livestock was wrecked on the reefs. Paul said he would like to get in on the hunt. We were told the wild pigs were very elusive, belligerent, and hard to catch in the thick, thorny brambles. But Paul said, "That's okay. Hotch and I are accomplished pig catchers. Hotch was the pig-catching champion of East St. Louis, Illinois."

The manager was very impressed.

"I got to the national finals," I said, modestly.

When we got to the thicket we were given our pig-catching equipment—a piece of fishnet with lead weights on the corners. "We can't use firearms," the manager said, "because there will be several of us in there and we can't run the risk of shooting each other."

Paul and I took our nets and went into the brambles, which were taller than we were, with thorns as long and as sharp as pencils. As we started to follow a narrow path, two pigs zipped across it like streaks of light.

"Holy shit," I said. "The East St. Louis champ ain't never gonna net one of those piggers."

"Don't give up, champ," Paul said. "We've got to outsmart 'em."

"How? You got a lasso?"

"The old fox is going to outfox 'em."

We crept along the path and could hear the pigs grousing in the underbrush. It was hot as hell in the airless thicket. "You hear that?" I said. "Listen to 'em—they're laughing at us."

"Yeah, but we're going to have the last laugh." Paul took some breakfast bread and a little jar of marmalade out of his pocket. He piled the bread thick with marmalade and laid it on the path. "Okay, Hotch, here's the deal. You go hide in the brush on that side, I'll be on this side, so once we get a piggy slurping up the bait, I'll scare him toward you and, being the champ you are, you can throw the net over him and get all the glory."

"Wait a minute—how the devil do you net a pig? No, listen, I'll scare him and *you* do the netting."

"Hotch, are you going to chicken out?"

"No, I'm going to pig out."

"Look, it's my brainstorm. I borrowed the bread and jam. The least you can do is slap your net around the sucker."

We took up our positions and waited. We could hear the club manager and her assistants working another part of the brush. I had my net raised in front of me, hanging down to the ground. I had absolutely no confidence in my ability to snatch a pig, in the unlikely event that we could corner one. The marmalade was attracting a variety of insects but not one curious pig.

"Paul," I whispered, "this is like going on a snipe hunt. I'm turning in my net." As I said it a plump little pig appeared on the path, eased up to the bread, and began to chomp on it. Paul suddenly darted out of the brush shouting, "Piggy! Piggy! Piggy!" and the alarmed pig, instead of dashing toward me with my quivering net, charged right at Paul, knocking him backwards and entangling the two of them in the net. I was laughing so hard that I had trouble closing the net around the pig and freeing Paul.

"Oink! Oink! Oink!" I called out, which was the prearranged signal for a catch. The manager and her staff appeared and congratulated me for having captured the pig. Paul had disentangled himself from the brambles by now and was laughing at me, basking in my moment of triumph.

"Hotchner, you slut," he said, "this is the last pig hunt I ever go on with you."

THAT NIGHT THERE was an alert that Rock Sound was in the path of a hurricane, which was expected to hit in full force by early afternoon of the following day if it continued on its present course. Paul said he was obligated to be back in New York and hoped the Pan Am plane would be in and out before the hurricane arrived.

By noon the following day the hurricane sent its calling card— high winds that bent the palms, a darkening sky, and slashing rain. Paul and I were in the airport waiting room with our bags, and he was pacing nervously, searching the sky for the Pan Am plane.

"Paul," I said, "give it up. Look at what's blowing out there. We ain't going nowhere."

"Oh yes we are," he said, as the jet broke through the heavy clouds and made a rough landing. It taxied in and discharged passengers who were buffeted as they came down the steps and struggled across the tarmac. A section of the fuselage skin had torn loose and was hanging beneath the windows. There was an announcement over the loudspeaker that there would be no passenger service to New York until further notice.

Paul went to see the airport manager, who was conferring with the plane's pilots. I tagged along. The airport manager said that Pan Am control in Miami had requested that the plane take off immediately if it was at all possible in order to avert the risk that it would be destroyed by the hurricane if it were on the ground. The Rock Sound airport did not have a hangar, and even if it had, it would likely have been destroyed too.

"What do you say, John?" the airport manager said to the pilot.

"I don't know, Harold. That's a nasty blow out there, a lot of wind shear, and there's that piece hanging off the fuselage."

"What about that, Billy?" the manager said to a skinny guy in Pan Am overalls.

"Well," he said, scratching his ear, "I guess we could do it up. It's just decoration anyway."

"Okay, I guess," the pilot said.

"I got to round up my crew," Billy said.

"How long will that take? We've got to do it fast if we're going to take off."

"We'll help him," Paul said, "won't we, Hotch?"

So that's how come we went out in that howler with the manager and the two pilots and Billy, who mounted a device that elevated him up to the ripped section. He held it back in place and then we zipped off sections from a large roll of duct tape and handed them up to Billy, who reattached the torn section. When he finished, the pilot said, "Well, I guess that'll do. We don't need to gas up. We better get out of here, toot sweet."

Paul said we'd be right out with our bags but the manager shook his head. "No passengers allowed."

Paul produced a sheet of paper on which he had written a statement that he now read: "We are on Pan Am flight 264 of our own volition, and absolve Pan Am of any and all responsibility for our passage."

Paul signed the paper and handed it to the manager as he grabbed his bag and headed for the plane. The manager was studying the paper. "Well, I don't think I can . . . I have to call Miami . . ."

I found myself following Paul through the hurricane's howling precursor, but as he started up the steps I shouted at him that I had decided to stay.

"Get your ass up here, Hotchnik," he yelled. "If we go down, I'm not swimming to Florida by myself."

The cabin door was bolted behind us and the plane started to taxi, just the two of us in this vast, empty, shuddering 747.

Paul was euphoric, just the kind of high drama that appealed to him. He went to the cockpit and positioned himself behind the pilots as they revved the jets and careened down the runway. As we took off, the wind badgered us and tossed us erratically like some of the jetsam that was floating around us. I had flown in pretty bad turbulence when I was in the air force, but those were baby turbulences compared to this. The plane was creaking and groaning and stuff was pelting against the windows. I felt like I was in *Dr. Strangelove*.

Paul staggered back to the cabin, enjoying himself, big grin on his face, holding on to the pitching seats. "Is the intrepid pig hunter having any fun?" he shouted.

"Fuck you, Newman," I said as my head bounced off the overhead baggage compartment.

Over the course of his career, Paul was involved in a number of film projects that didn't come to fruition, and there were two in particular that he especially pursued but, try as he did, he couldn't make happen. In the 1970s he took an option on a novel called *The Front Runner*, a best seller about a coach who falls in love with the best runner on his men's track team. Paul wanted to play the coach but no studio would back a film, even with Paul starring, that depicted a love affair between two men. Also every actor whom Paul contacted to play the track star turned him down. It was a taboo that Hollywood was not yet ready to defy. It took *Brokeback Mountain*, many years later, to overcome that taboo.

Paul's other pet project was *The Tin Lizzy Troop*, a comic novel by Glendon Swarthout. Paul acquired film rights, intending to write the screenplay (his first attempt) and direct. *Tin Lizzy* is about a mounted cavalry unit in 1916 that was dispatched to the Mexico-Texas border to capture Pancho Villa's bandits who had raided a U.S. outpost. Attached to that cavalry unit was a group of Model Ts, driven by six effete members of the Philadelphia Light Horse, a posh military club to which only socially and financially upper-crust gentlemen were elected. The book follows these men and their Tin Lizzies as they pursue the enemy, under the command of a hard-nosed U.S. Cavalry officer.

All one summer Paul worked on writing the screenplay, enjoying himself enormously. He sometimes gave me a scene to read, or read one to me. He never asked me for input nor did I volunteer any. Paul was especially fond of the opening scene, which certainly was inventive and humorous. I never read the entire script from beginning to end, only disjointed scenes.

In the fall, Paul circulated his script to major studios and independent producers, but there were no takers. He even offered to perform as well as direct, but it didn't help. He expressed his frustration to me many times, puzzled as to why the studios didn't go for the comic encounters of the Tin Lizzy Troop with the bandits. My theory was that Paul had created good individual scenes that were not effectively connected and that there wasn't an arc to the screenplay, a bridge that could carry those scenes to a rousing finish.

PAUL WAS VERY selective about which of the countless number of scripts submitted to him, he chose. "Of all the scripts I've turned down," Paul told me, "the only two I regret are *Jaws,* because I didn't think they could make a Hollywood fake shark believable, and *All That Jazz,* because it called for dancing and I couldn't dance. A year later, however, I discovered I could dance, but they were already filming."

ABOUT THE SAME time that Paul gave up on the Tin Lizzies, he had to give up on our project, *After the Storm.* I had finished reworking the script, incorporating material from our trip, and we had looked forward to returning to the Bahamas to make the film, but it didn't happen. I received a call from Phil Feldman, who was the administrative executive of First Artists; he invited me to lunch to talk about *After the Storm.* Paul wasn't there. Phil had bad news. First Artists had come unraveled because of infighting between the superstar members, mostly because they were devoting their best efforts to the projects of traditional major filmmakers and only bringing their lesser projects to First Artists. It was the same fissure that had split

United Artists, with charges and countercharges between Douglas Fairbanks and Charlie Chaplin. Mary Pickford, it seems, stayed demurely above the fray. Hollywood executives moved in and took control of United Artists, which ultimately found its footing without the involvement of the founding superstars.

This did not happen to First Artists. Phil explained that the contractual ramifications were such that First Artists had become a jumble of lawyers with no settlement in sight.

"So what happens to *After the Storm*?" I asked.

"Nothing. It was the property of First Artists as were several other projects, but none of those assets can be activated until all the legal matters are resolved—and God knows when that will happen, if ever."

"So that's that."

"I'm sorry, Hotch. I know Paul is all set on it, but I can't do a thing about it."

TWENTY-FIVE YEARS later I reworked a watered-down version of *After the Storm* as a network special on an inadequate budget, with Benjamin Bratt playing the part intended for Paul. All I could do was fantasize about what could have been.

*P*aul was directing a movie in Bridgeport, Connecticut, a depressed, crime-ridden, industrial town fifteen minutes from Westport. The movie, *The Effect of Gamma Rays on Man-in-the-Moon Marigolds*, was based on a Pulitzer Prize–winning play by Paul Zindel that Paul and Joanne saw in New York and acquired as a starring vehicle for Joanne. Their first collaboration, *Rachel, Rachel*, had been a success artistically and financially, and they hoped to repeat that success with *Gamma Rays*. The play concerned frustrated, morose, middle-aged Beatrice Hunsdorfer, a single mother raising two teenage daughters, the younger one intelligent and ambitious, the other morose and confused. The Newmans' daughter Nell was cast in the role of Beatrice's younger daughter; Eli Wallach's daughter Roberta was the other daughter. The set for the Hunsdorfer house had been constructed inside an abandoned Hungarian church.

Joanne immersed herself in the sordid drabness of her environment and the spiteful, cruel, despondent hopelessness of Beatrice.

Being so close to Bridgeport, I visited the film's location several times during the weeks they were shooting, and each time I was impressed by the way Joanne had increasingly invested herself with the horribleness of Beatrice Hunsdorfer. She had cut her hair and dyed it a drab mousy color, and her makeup and clothes accentuated the self-loathing essence of her character. Even her exchanges with

Paul, which had been so quiet and respectful during the filming of *Rachel, Rachel* (I had gone to Bethel, Connecticut, a couple of times and watched them at work on that film), were quite the opposite for *Gamma Rays*. Joanne retained the belligerence of Beatrice in her sometimes heated exchanges with Paul over differences in interpretations of scenes and dialogue. Joanne wanted a little humor and compassion to shine through the repulsiveness, but Paul felt that there was nothing in the script that would lend itself to that. And, as she later admitted, for the first time in her career as an actress, Joanne took her loathsome persona home with her, so that she was the same Beatrice Hunsdorfer with her own family as she was with her make-believe one.

"I was possessed by demons," she said. "I was so depressed and suicidal during that film I couldn't stand it. I came close to sheer insanity. It's the one picture I wish I hadn't done. It had a terrible effect on me. That picture left scars."

One night, rather late, I heard a car come crunching up my gravel driveway. I flipped on the outside lights. Paul got out of his car, carrying a shopping bag with his clothes in it.

"Hotchkin," he said, "I'd like to occupy your spare room. If I spend another night in bed with Beatrice Hunsdorfer, one of us will not be on the set tomorrow."

One of the things that nurtured our friendship was the fact that we didn't take ourselves seriously. Or each other. We were both in unrealistic make-believe professions. As a fiction writer and playwright I indulged my memories and fantasies; the more unbuttoned my imagination, the more successful the fantasy. Paul always maintained that the best actors, including himself, were the ones who preserved the child within them, performing as they do with makeup and costumes and toy guns and all the other make-believes of their childhoods. Butch Cassidy doing his giddy acrobatics on that bicycle; using too much dynamite on the train's safe and raining money down on everyone's head; staging bank holdups in Bolivia while struggling with the language; eating all those eggs in *Cool Hand Luke*; pulling off the phony card game in *The Sting*; handling the puck in *Slap Shot*; nabbing the bad guys in *Fort Apache the Bronx*—all examples of Paul's ability to make juvenile fantasies into movie realities.

To keep himself loose and pliable and imbued with the mischievousness that nourished him, Paul often resorted to practical jokes. George Roy Hill told me about some of the practical jokes that Paul played on him. During the filming of *Slap Shot*, Paul staged a fake car crash with himself behind the wheel of one of the wrecked cars, causing George to race to the crash site fearful of what had happened to Paul, who emerged with a big smile on his face. It was George's refusal to stand a round of drinks for the crew (George was a notorious tightwad) that motivated Paul to stage that crash.

Another occurred during the filming of *Butch Cassidy*. Paul had tried to convince George to make some changes in a particular scene, but George was intractable. To get even, Paul had George's desk sawed in half—causing it to collapse in George's lap when he sat down at it.

Paul duped George for a third time during *The Sting*. This joke was occasioned by George's refusal to consider an alternate ending that Paul had proposed. When shooting ended and George left the wrap party to get his car, he found that his Chevy had been cut in half. George ignored the bisected Chevy, calmly picked up the phone, and called a cab to take him to his hotel. When he got there, Paul was standing at the entrance dangling a set of keys, which he handed to George. A gleaming new sports car stood at the curb.

"Here's your new car, George," Paul said. "You needed an upgrade."

PAUL PULLED IDENTICAL practical jokes on two of his directors: John Huston during the making of *The Mackintosh Man* and Otto Preminger while filming *Exodus*. In the case of *Mackintosh Man*, Huston's affront was that he had paid no attention to Paul's lengthy list of script suggestions. With the cameras rolling on a fight scene being played sixty feet above ground, Paul hurled a look-alike dummy through a window. It landed with a thud, causing Huston to yell "Cut!" and race to the scene.

The same joke was even more effective when Paul sprung it on Preminger during a pivotal scene in *Exodus*. Preminger, a humorless, vindictive man, not only had rejected Paul's list of script suggestions but had also lectured Paul on why an actor's suggestions were never helpful. During a pivotal scene, Paul was engaged in a bloody fight on the top balcony of a high-rise building; a perfect look-alike dummy had been adroitly substituted for him. The script called for Paul to knock out the villain. But now Preminger, directing from a unit on the ground, saw the villain knock "Paul" off the balcony, the dummy spinning downward and landing with an ominous splat. Preminger was so shaken that he collapsed and required first aid.

PAUL AND ROBERT REDFORD had a collegial but prickly relationship, as illustrated by their exchange of practical jokes. Redford fired the first salvo when, as a birthday present for Paul, he had a junkyard Porsche, sans wheels and fenders, put in Paul's driveway with a big blue ribbon around it.

Paul showed me the pathetic Porsche and then described his plan of reprisal. He had engaged a compacting company to pick up the Porsche and turn it into a metal lump. Paul had located the real estate agent who had brokered Redford's Westport house. In exchange for an autographed picture, the broker opened Redford's front door for the compactors, who deposited the Porsche lump in the middle of Redford's living room with Redford's blue ribbon securely around it.

I HAD DINNER one evening with Paul and Robert Altman, who had directed him in *Buffalo Bill and the Indians*. They reminisced about the good times they had making the film, drinking beer, smoking a little pot, and improvising on camera.

Altman also described how one of Paul's practical jokes had backfired. During filming Paul had snuck three hundred live chickens into Altman's trailer to greet him when he returned that evening. Altman did not return, however, but spent the night elsewhere. By the time he did return the following day, the three hundred chickens had suffocated in the heat, and the clinging putrefaction of the dead chickens necessitated replacing Altman's trailer with a new one at Paul's expense.

There was one practical joke, however, that Paul directed at Altman which did work. Altman had hosted a dinner for Paul and other members of the cast and had served a very cheap wine that was barely drinkable.

The following day, a goat was delivered to Altman on the set of *Buffalo Bill and the Indians*, interrupting the filming. The goat had this note attached to the collar around his neck, a note that was read aloud: "Dear Bob, Since what you serve at dinner is goat piss you may as well have one handy."

*P*aul and Joanne spent numerous weekends in search of a desirable cemetery for their burial plots. The excursions included overnights at country inns that had been researched by Joanne in authoritative Baedekers. Paul and Joanne loved these cemetery tours and were effusive about the grand old country inns where they stayed. After a while, as I recall, they narrowed their selection down to a graveyard in New Hampshire that dated back to the revolutionary war, and one in upstate Connecticut that was perched above a verdant valley.

I once asked Paul why he was being so particular about the site of their interment.

"Because we're going to be there for a long, long time," Paul said, "and it would be nice if we were in beautiful surroundings: dogwoods and hyacinths, red maples and hydrangeas."

Time passed, and one day it occurred to me that I did not know which heavenly spot they had chosen for their eternal resting place.

"So, Paul, which spot did you choose?"

"Neither."

"Have you made a different choice?"

"Yes."

"What?"

"Cremation."

January 26, 1975, was Paul's fiftieth birthday, and he celebrated the occasion with proper pomp and ceremony. He had assembled his five daughters at his house on Coleytown Road. The temperature was in the low twenties but, as was his custom, Paul appeared for breakfast in swim trunks and bathrobe. Joanne and the girls sat at the breakfast table and watched from the window as Paul went down to the Aspetuck River that ran through his property. Peeling off his bathrobe he dived into the freezing water and swam vigorously for fifteen minutes before reclaiming his robe and joining his breakfast ladies.

Lunch that day was confined to Joanne and the girls, but that evening fifty of us were invited to a New York restaurant, La Cave Henri VI, for a celebration. George Roy Hill, Robert Redford, Eli Wallach and Anne Jackson, the writer Stewart Stern, Gene Shalit, the ballet master Edward Villella, Patricia Neal, Joe Mankowitz, Fred Coe, Marty Ritt, Shirley MacLaine, and Lauren Bacall were among the invitees. There was a succession of ribald toasts, and Neil Sedaka played a few of his songs that Sammy Cahn had gussied up with special lyrics. Redford's present was the junkyard Porsche that had been delivered to Paul's driveway in Westport earlier in the day.

The food was good, the wine better, and the affection for Paul pronounced. Actors and production people from some of his movies were present, wearing T-shirts and jackets identifying the flicks they

By the time he reached his sixtieth birthday, Paul had recovered his joie de vivre.

had worked on. A producer from *Somebody Up There Likes Me* presented Paul with the boxing gloves he had used in the movie. I gave him a gadget called "The Fish Finder—guaranteed to attract the most elusive fish in your vicinity." His kids gave him a wicker wheelchair and someone contributed a case of Coors. It was a festive evening, but knowing Paul as I did, I thought he was rather subdued, only half risen to the occasion.

I think that fifty was more than a number for Paul. I think it triggered reflection and longing and appraisal of those fifty years and what might lie ahead. After fifty, Paul became less introverted and more exposed to openly involving himself in things that had meaning for him.

MARIO'S IS AN old-time Italian restaurant opposite the Westport railroad station, a celebrated institution noted for its bold pastas and the long mahogany bar that has nurtured generations of evening commuters with emergency martinis before their trek home. For Paul and me it was our favorite lunch spot, not for martinis but for hamburgers and beer.

"There's nothing like an Italian burger," Paul said, as he slathered ketchup and mustard on his and sliced his pickle into bite-size pieces.

"What do you mean, an Italian burger? It's just a big, juicy burger."

"I don't know what they do to it, but it tastes Italian."

I decided not to pursue that one.

"Do you know how many times we were out in the boat last summer?" Paul asked, as he grunted approvingly over his first bite of hamburger.

"How many?"

"Twice. Pretty awful, don't you think?"

"I tried but you were always busy with one thing or another. The summer passed me by same as you."

"We've got to turn it around, Hotch. How many books and plays have you written?"

"I don't know—a dozen I guess."

"Well I counted up last night. I've done forty-eight movies since 1954—that's more than two every year, and how many are any good? Maybe half a dozen. Looking back at what I've done, twenty-five years, I've decided I don't really like acting anymore. I read four, five scripts a week, nothing there that makes me want to get up and go. These last movies, I just went through the motions. All the tricks I've learned, I just repeated them. Nothing new to pull out of myself. Sweat a little, die a little—the way it was with *Hustler* and *Hud* . . . *Hombre* . . . *Cool Hand* . . . all those H's made me think H's brought me luck. That's why I got them to change the name of the detective from Archer to Harper. The film turned out okay but anything would have been a tonic after *Lady L*, that turkey I made with Sophia Loren. She radiated icicles. Showed up on the set when she felt like it, all work and no fun. We didn't exchange ten words other than the ones in the script. The director was delightful, Peter Ustinov. He sat us down and, in an attempt to improve our frigid love scenes, suggested we get to know each other a little better. So the next morning when Sophia comes on the set she looks at me and says, 'Paul, what do they use to attach your mustache?' I said, 'Sperm,' which really put the frost on the enchilada. Actually, my mustache was part of the problem. Did you see *Lady L*? No? Well, very few did. My character was a romancing French anarchist, someone I could never play properly. Every day while they were making me up with my fake curly mustache and my thick sappy wig, I prayed some catastrophe would derail the film, other than the catastrophe of my performance."

"I wrote a play when I felt like that," I said. "After fifty pages I knew I had no juice for it, but there were commitments involving others . . . Of course it was a flop."

"You know, to be honest, I don't think I have a passion for acting anymore. Only passion I have is for racing. Doesn't matter if it's me racing or if I'm in the pit with my team, I think about it all week. It's all I really care about. I've tried to get involved with politics, but there's no one who has real leadership I can get excited about, nothing that makes me want to care. I don't really have the desire to direct anymore. *Rachel* was okay but *Sometimes a Great Notion* was heavy lifting and *Gamma Rays* was a real downer. Of course, if I could find a script with the clout of *Cool Hand Luke*, that might restart my motor, but . . . *Luke* was an original. That's what I need, an original, otherwise I'm just repeating myself. The more movies I make, the more I repeat myself. I just do what I've done before. I like having to dig inside myself to create something. Like I did in *The Battler*, becoming that pathetically deranged boxer. That was a real kick. Well . . . the kick's gone out of it for me. I'm going to take a year off. No scripts to read. None of that. Just racing, going out in the boat, maybe take Joanne and the kids on a bicycle tour of Europe— something like that. A year off, maybe I'll find something new that grabs me. Something with some real life to it. A challenge. That's what racing is for me. I hunker down in the driver's seat and my adrenaline perks way up because there's thirty guys hunkered down in their racers wanting to beat me to the checkered flag."

The waitress came to clear our dishes and ask if we wanted coffee.

"Yes," Paul said, "coffee and the cream of life."

"I've only got half-and-half, dearie," the waitress said.

"Paul," I said, "I'll bet you can't last a year."

"You're on. Twenty-five-cent bet. Look, Hotch, I've hit fifty now, and you've got a few years on me, we don't have a hell of a lot of time to do something, something else, something that matters, something makes me want to get up in the morning."

"I hear you, but don't belittle what you've done. Wonderful films. They'll be around for a long time and they've entertained a ton of people."

"But we can do more. I belong to an environmental group that's trying to keep acres of pristine land from a developer's bulldozers. I

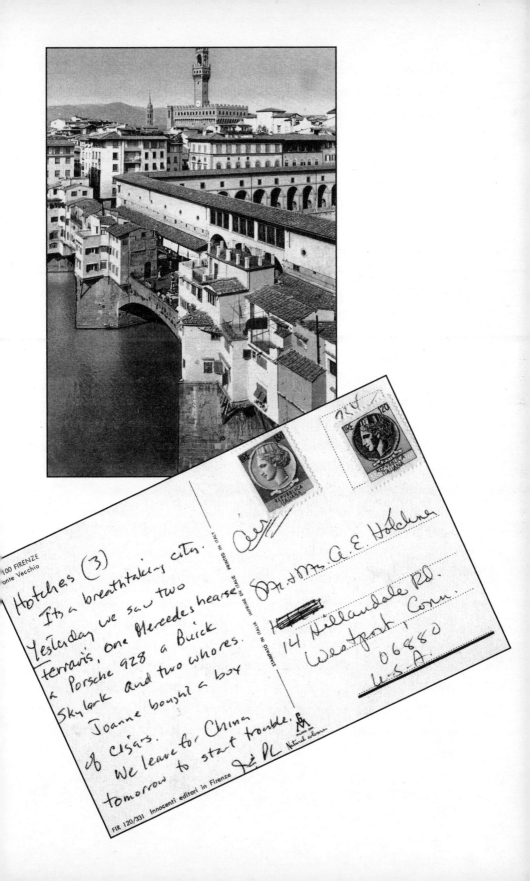

100 FIRENZE
onte Vecchio

Hotches (3)
   It's a breathtaking city.
Yesterday we saw two
Ferraris, one Mercedes hearse,
a Porsche 928, a Buick
Skylark and two whores.
   Joanne bought a box
of cigars.
   We leave for China
tomorrow to start trouble.   Je & PL

FIR 120/331 Innocenti editori in Firenze

Mr. & Mrs. A. E. Hotchner
14 Hillandale Rd.
Westport, Conn.
          06880
          U.S.A.

feel better about that than movies right now. Look, I've gained a certain amount of recognition. I'm a celebrity—awful word—I should be using that, cashing in on it to do some good."

"Like what?"

"I just made a public service spot for television, urging drivers to buckle up their seat belts. If my face gets their attention and they see me stepping into my car, buckling up—maybe I'll get some people to pay attention. Save some lives. As long as I have to suffer paparazzi and autograph hounds and the little old ladies asking me to take off my sunglasses so they can see my eyes, then I should put that to good use. And I will. I've been lucky and I want that luck to go beyond Lady Ls and Lime Rock finishes."

"I think we both owe a lot to Lady Luck, if she is a lady."

"Well, for me I'd have to say that luck has been the most important element of my life. I'm not religious, I don't believe in mysticism or heavenly beings, but I firmly believe in luck, good and bad. For me, being lucky starts when you have a good sperm ride that makes a good womb connection that produces lucky genes. Genes that don't have defects that will get in your way. That's pure luck. And as you live, you learn that luck is an art, the art of being able to recognize luck when it goes by you—walks by you, or runs by you— and you don't let it pass you by. Grab it and you are lucky. True luck is not holding the best cards but knowing just when to quit and go home. Good luck is sitting on a sofa on a movie set, as I did, and as you get up and step away from the sofa, a massive light fixture from a ceiling track comes crashing down and lands on the exact spot you just vacated. Good luck is having a fabulous woman in your life for twenty years. I didn't let her pass me by. I grabbed her and held her and that was great good luck. When you grab a passing script that you know you should let go and it turns out to be a bomb, that's bad luck because you brought it on yourself. I keep a quotation handy that says it for me."

In the queer mess of human destiny the determining factor is
Luck. For every important place in life there are many men of fairly
equal capacities. Among them Luck divides who shall accomplish
the great work, who shall be crowned with laurel, and who shall
fall back in obscurity and silence.—*William E. Woodward*

The demand for our dressing was so great, we were kept prisoners in the basement.

otchnik, how about coming over and giving me a hand with something."

"When?"

"Now. You busy?"

That's how it started. Innocently enough. It is a couple of days before Christmas, a light snow falling, houses bedecked with wreaths and lights, smoke from fireplaces redolent in the air. I drive through his automated gates and look for Paul in the converted barn. I find him under the barn in a space that had once been a stable for farm horses. He is standing in the middle of the dirt floor surrounded by a bewildering collection of objects: an empty washtub; a bucket with Budweisers nestled in ice; an array of bottles of olive oil, vinegar, mustard and other condiments; a large collection of old bottles that have been somewhat sanitized. There are two wooden stools and a canoe paddle is leaning against a wall of crumbling cement and active cobwebs. There are two horse stalls, long vacated, but the faint aroma of horses and desiccated manure fragments still remain along with the hovels of various field animals who bunk there.

"Grab a beer," Paul said, "and let's get to work."

"On what?" I said as I popped the tab on a Budweiser.

"My salad dressing."

More than his acting, more than his racing, Paul was proudest of his salad dressing, a blend of olive oil, red wine vinegar, and a variety of herbs and spices. Many's the time we would be dining in a fashionable restaurant and Paul would ask the waiter to bring his salad without any dressing, along with the ingredients he needed to make his own at the table. I was with him on one such occasion when a waiter made the mistake of serving Paul's salad with the restaurant's dressing. Paul got up, took the salad to the men's room, washed off the dressing, dried the salad with paper towels, returned to the table, and proceeded to use his own ingredients—which by then had been brought to the table. When Paul's children went away to school, he always made sure they took some of his salad dressing that he had bottled for them.

"Here's the drill. We'll mix up a big batch of my dressing in this tub, fill all these bottles, punch in these corks, and slap on these stickers."

The stickers read: Newman's Own Dressing.

"And just what are we to do with all these bottles once we fill 'em, cork 'em, and label 'em?"

"Our two families will go house to house and sing carols and give a bottle to every house as a Christmas present. Oh, one more thing—we tie these red ribbons around the necks of the bottles."

"What makes you think the neighbors will be thrilled with your dressing?"

"You ever taste the stuff that Kraft and Wishbone and the others put in their bottles—sugar, artificial coloring, chemical preservatives, gums—poison like that. So when the neighbors sprinkle Newman's Own on their Christmas salads, they will be borne up to salad heaven."

Paul had no idea what quantities were needed for such a large batch of his elixir, so he unceremoniously dumped six bottles of olive oil, twelve bottles of red wine vinegar, six boxes of pepper, a large dose of salt, and handfuls of the assembled herbs. Then he handed me the paddle, which obviously came from the canoe he paddled on the Aspetuck River.

"Okay, Hotch, as I add my stuff to the mix you begin to stir with a counter-clockwise motion, nice and easy so it doesn't froth."

I leaned over the washtub and began to stir Paul's concoction. The paddle didn't look very clean to me but Paul believed that the olive oil combined with the vinegar produced a hygienic effect, obviating the need to be concerned about sanitation.

"Hotch, you are not counter-clocking. You are *frothing* the mix!"

"I am *not* frothing! Show me frothing."

"You are pulling it straight toward you. You've got to go with the paddle."

"I am! I'm giving the paddle everything I've got."

"Waffle it, gyrate it, go with the paddle."

"I am! I am! I've had three beers and if I go any further with the paddle I'm going to fall facedown in your soup."

"That's okay, just as long as it isn't buttfirst."

A few times during our hours of labor, someone would show up at the entrance. Caroline the housekeeper, or Joanne, or one of the kids, but they were stopped in their tracks by the smell of old horse piss and mold commingled with beer fumes and the aroma of the salad-dressing ingredients. After a deep breath, all of the interlopers beat immediate retreats.

After we had filled and corked and labeled all the bottles, a quantity of dressing remained in the tub.

"What a pity," Paul said, clearly dismayed that any of his elixir might go to waste.

"Goodwill will not take salad dressing," I said.

"Tell you what," Paul said, his pinched face brightening. "I'll get a couple more bottles, let's fill 'em and maybe a few delis and upscale food stores will sell them. We can make a few bucks—Newman's Own holiday hustle."

"What'll we charge?"

"How about six bucks?"

"Forget it."

"There you go! Always the killjoy."

"It's against the law."

"What's against the law?"

"Look at this place, crawlies all over it. Bugs fly in here and immediately keel over. Somebody buys one of these Newman's Owns in its unwashed bottle and—"

"I rinsed all the bottles!"

"—croaks, you'll be in court without liability insurance, maybe in handcuffs. You could wind up without your basement and everything above it. I happen to recall from my brief lawyer career that the government is finicky about enforcing its rules and regulations. Hygiene, labels, ingredients, all that rigmarole."

"Fine!" Paul said, not a bit daunted. "Let's do it. An okay label, a sexy bottle, someone to bottle it, and see if we can make a buck or two."

And that's how our baby was born—not in a manger but in a washtub—not a wise man in sight.

One of the advantages of being Paul Newman was the power that his name commanded. "Paul Newman calling" dissolved barriers, brought down the walls of Jericho. So when Paul learned that the Marketing Corporation of America, the largest marketing corporation in the country, was headquartered in Westport, he called the president and asked for a meeting to discuss his bottle of salad dressing. The president was pleased to schedule an appointment immediately.

That's how it happened that we were in the very impressive MCA conference room with the president and five of his department heads, all them there, I suspect, to see the movie star, not the pathetic bottle of salad dressing that Paul placed on the table before him, a bottle that had once contained ketchup.

"Now as I understand it, this is a salad dressing of your concoction, Mr. Newman," the president said, "that you would like to market in the U.S. of A. Well, we can do for you what we do for the big brands—Libby's, Heinz, Del Monte, Campbell's, Kraft—when they launch a new product."

I was embarrassed that our miserable bottle of washtub dressing that I had gyrated with an unsanitary canoe paddle is being considered alongside food products produced by the biggest companies in the country. I felt like an imposter, but Paul was enjoying this encounter because he honestly felt that his dressing was superior to anything produced by any of these food giants.

"First of all," the president was saying, "you have to feel the public's pulse to determine how they react to your dressing."

I had a mental glimpse of the president's fingers on the humongous wrist of the U.S. of A.

"We would dispatch people across the country to gather focus groups of varied ethnicity, financial strata, age groups, sexual preference, fast-food habits, footwear use or non-use, deodorants, the whole load. We would go around the country, asking folks in shopping malls and such places how they like the bottle, the name, the taste—we'd have them sample it on lettuce, tomatoes, onions, cabbage, sausage. Then the price—you have to set a price for us—questions like that, and then in maybe seven or eight sections of the country we'd correlate the results and study them to let you know how to adjust all those things to maximize your introductory impact."

"What would that cost?" Paul asked.

"Depending on the focus depth, somewhere between three hundred and four hundred thousand dollars. Now once you're ready to roll out the product, you'll have to learn how to attend to distribution, promotion, and advertising, public relations. Our experience is with the big guys—Heinz, Kraft, etcetera—and they figure to spend a million dollars to launch a new product. That's the general rule the first year. We'll teach you how to muscle into the big stores. You'll have to make deals, especially with outfits like A&P and Kroger's—discounts, two-for-ones, free stuff, just to get your bottle on the shelf—and then how to avoid winding up on the bottom shelf, down below the packed rows of Krafts and Wishbones, which have all the eye-level spaces. The odds on new products are about the same as roulette. Even the biggest companies have had expensive failures—Campbell's refrigerated soups, Gerber's 'adult' food line, Nabisco's giant-size Oreo cookies. And then there's the history of celebrity products—which Karen will tell you about."

"Celebrity products fall into a category of their own," said

Karen, a trim blonde in a tailored suit. "That doesn't refer to fictional characters like Aunt Jemima, Betty Crocker, and Sara Lee. Nor does it mean endorsers, like the sport stars that appear on Wheaties boxes. But celebrities who come out with their own products—Rocky Graziano's spaghetti sauce, Mickey Mantle's barbecue sauce, Nolan Ryan's All-Star Fruit Snacks, Gloria Vanderbilt's salad dressing, Reggie Jackson's candy bar, Carl Yastrzemski's Big Yaz bread, Diane von Furstenberg's facial tissue, Bill Blass's chocolates, Polly Bergen's Oil-of-the-Turtle cosmetics, Marilyn Monroe's merlot, Fess Parker's wine, James Darren's spaghetti sauce, Phyllis Diller's Philli Dilli Chili, Richard Simmons's Salad Spray, Tommy Lasorda's spaghetti sauce, Yves Saint Laurent's cigarettes, Frank Sinatra's neckties—all failures. Take Graziano, for example. He was a popular prizefighter, middle-weight champ, big fights with Tony Zale, and as an entertainment personality he appeared in a series of television shows—all kinds of sitcoms and whatnot. Rocky promoted the hell out of his sauce, but after an initial surge, it simply died and dropped off the shelves— shoppers bought one jar out of curiosity and that was it. There's never been a celebrity success in the food business. We estimate the total start-up loss for celebrity products somewhere close to nine hundred million dollars."

I slid down in my chair.

"Now don't be too discouraged by all of this," the president said, as he saw my chin down on my chest. "There's always a first time. But no one can predict public response. Politics, automobiles, fashion, music, name it—it's a crap shoot. But if we canvass our focus groups and we adjust your product to respond to it, and if you have the capital to get through the losses of the first year, I'd say the odds would be fifty-five to forty-five against flopping."

"No offense, Mr. Newman," Karen said, "but just because they liked you as Butch Cassidy doesn't mean they'll like your salad dressing."

"Maybe we should call it Redford's Own."

"They wouldn't like it any better."

"I'd have someone to blame."

We thanked them for their time and said we'd think it over. We said nothing on the walk across the parking lot to Newman's Volkswagen, the rear seat of which had been removed to accommodate a small-block Ford V-8.

"So let's add it up," I said, as we sat in the idling Volks. "Four hundred thou for all those focus groups, a million to lose the first year, looks like one million four hundred thousand dollars to me. I don't think my checkbook can handle my share of that."

"Okay, tell you what," Paul said. "We'll gather a dozen of our friends and have a blind taste-testing. We'll put all the big name brands in numbered saucers, ours in the mix, and have them rated from one to ten. Then let's you and me put up twenty thousand dollars each, and when that's gone we go out of business."

Paul put the Volkswagen in gear and took off at his usual ninety miles an hour. "I feel pretty good," he said, "don't you? We just saved one million three hundred and sixty thousand dollars."

$\mathcal{W}$e decided to visit the local Stop & Shop supermarket
to take a look at our competition. We recoiled at the sight of the
salad-dressing section. A solid glass wall of every conceivable kind of
dressing: a dozen different Krafts, another dozen Wishbones, plus
Hidden Valley, Marzetti's, Henry and Henry, Bernstein's, and countless
others. As Paul read the content labels, however, it was apparent that
they all contained the same elements to preserve them: sweetness
in a variety of forms, artificial colorings, gums, other chemical
preservatives—all the elements that his all-natural dressing was
eliminating.

The possibility of putting a crack in this glass wall of salad
dressings was rather daunting, but then again, for Paul the challenge is
what made it interesting. Hustling his bottle of salad dressing was a
lark, an open-end adventure. David against those endless shelves of
Kraft and Wishbone Goliaths. We'd give it a shot, forty thousand
dollars' worth, but when it was spent we'd fold our tent, like when you
blow all your wad in Las Vegas and head for the exit. Our odds were
about the same as roulette, but what the hell—we'd get a bottler, make
a label, take out insurance, and let 'er rip.

A smiling man in a Stop & Shop jacket approached us. "May I
assist you, Mr. Newman? I'm Martin Orloff, the store manager."

"We were just looking at our competition," Paul said.

"Competition?"

"I'm bringing out my own dressing. How do you think it would do?"

"Depends."

"On what?"

"How much you promote it, what it costs, and if it's better than all of these."

A woman shopper, putting a bottle of Kraft dressing in her cart, chimed in: "I'd buy it Mr. Newman."

"Thank you—that's good to know."

"One time, so I could show it to my bridge club."

"Only once?"

"I'd have to try it on my salad. It's hard to believe that a movie star like you could make a dressing better than Kraft."

"I'd buy it regular," said a second shopper who had joined our group. "I love your movies and I'm sure I'd love your salad dressing. When does it come out?"

"Any day now."

Paul took a pen from Orloff's breast pocket and wrote down the shoppers' reactions. Then he moved along the salad-dressing aisle and put his question to other shoppers, writing down their responses. He returned the pen to Orloff, who walked us to the exit.

"Let me know in advance," Orloff said, "and I'll give you a thirty-day free slotting space."

When we got outside, Paul gave me his slip of paper. "There you are, Hotchnik, that's our four-hundred-thousand-dollar focus group."

"Not so fast," I said, "there's part two."

"Which is?"

"A focus group to taste the product. You said we'd gather a bunch of our friends and have a taste-off against all the name brands."

"So I did. Okay, I'll call Martha and see if we can use her place."

MARTHA STEWART AND her husband, Andy, ran a catering business out of their home on Turkey Hill Road, occasionally catering

Early Westport days: We scoured the woods for fireplace logs we then lugged to our houses.

Paul demonstrating how his delicious popcorn should be savored—one kernel at a time.

Hotch's sixtieth birthday party. Paul's present was this large wicker basket filled with layers of exotic hats, beer, and pornographic magazines.

Paul's unique technique for tossing a salad with his dressing.

Our trade secrets were closely guarded to keep them from Gene Shalit's ears.

Susie Seal expressing her gratitude for the Newman's Own donation to the Maritime Aquarium at Norwalk.

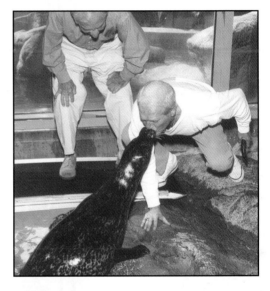

Two distinguished pastalogists: Dr. P. Linguini Newmanelli and Professor A. Espresso Hotchnissimo.

(Left) While drinking our lemonade during the making of this poster, Whoopi announced she could feel her virginity being restored.

(Below, left) During rehearsal we often invented action and dialogue on the spot. On this occasion, we decided Paul would play Tinkerbell with a cigar and a bottle of beer.

(Below) Camp gala 11: King Beer, garnished with Budweisers, with his ever-loving Queen Whoopi. Joan Rivers was Cordelia.

Camp gala 12: Cinderella (Julia Roberts), her fairy godmother (Nathan Lane), and Paul as her happy-go-lucky godfather who rode her to the ball on a motor scooter. This gala and the ones that followed each earned over a million dollars. The audiences came from New York, Connecticut, Massachusetts, and New Jersey.

Hotch reversed My Fair Lady to My Fair Laddie, starring Bruce Willis as Eli Doolittle, Meryl Streep as Professor Henrietta Higgins, Christine Baranski as Countess Pickering, and Paul as Alfred Doolittle, who drives a race car in the Grand Prix.

Paul's last camp gala, cavorting as Jack who broke his crown with Renée Zellweger as the Old Woman Who Lived in a Shoe. In their eighteen-year run, the galas played to 5,900 people and raised $11,187,490 million.

In the gala send-up of The Wizard of Oz, *Paul was the Cowardly Lion, afraid to drive top speed at the Indianapolis 500. The wonderful tap dancer Savion Glover was the Tin Man, and Tony Randall played the Scarecrow.*

(Below) Thankfully, Gilbert and Sullivan were not around to see Paul as Kokodoko in Hotch's butchering of The Mikado.

Paul in the place where he was happiest—with the campers at the Hole-in-the-Wall-Gang Camp.

He loved to bike to the dining hall and have lunch with the kids.

Paul said he would give the graduation address if Joanne managed to graduate from Sarah Lawrence—she did and he did.

The photographer asked them to look like serious businessmen, which obviously was a mistake.

dinner parties for us. She filled twenty bowls with samples of the leading brands, one with Newman's dressing. There were mounds of lettuce leaves to dip in the dressing, and glasses of water for palate cleansing. In addition, tasters were provided with pads to evaluate each dressing on a scale of one to ten. Paul and I agreed that if we didn't score near the top, we'd pack up and slink off.

The twenty friends we invited regarded this as a kind of party and took their sweet time dipping, chewing, cleansing, tabulating, and gossiping with the other tasters but, as instructed, not about their choices. Waiting for them to run the gamut of the bowls was like waiting for reviews on opening night in the theater.

Finally Martha announced the tabulation: eighteen had marked bowl number seven, Paul's baby, in first place. Martha said the only thing that could improve it was to put a bay leaf in every bottle. She asked Paul what he was calling his dressing.

"Salad King—I'll be the salad king of New England."

"And I'll be the court jester," I said.

The following day, Paul's attorney, Leo Nevas, incorporated us as the Salad King Corporation, using his office as the corporation's address. He also filed for a copyright on "Salad King." We didn't have a bottle or a label or insurance, but we did have titles—P. L. Newman, president, and A. E. Hotchner, vice president of Salad King, Inc.

A few days later, Martha called Paul. "I've been thinking about that name Salad King. Kings have always put their name in their titles, like King Paul the First."

"No," Paul said, "this dressing is not for royalty, it's for commoners. How about Newman's Own? It's left over from the restaurant Hotch and I didn't open."

"More like it," Martha said. "I'll be glad to use it on salads at the dinners I cater."

*F*inding someone to bottle our dressing was the highest hurdle we had to jump. We heard of a gentleman vintner in upstate Connecticut who had a small vineyard and bottled the white wine he produced. We drove up to see his operation, but his assembly line consisted of five teenagers who came in after school. One of them filled the bottles, one by one, from the spigot on the cask, another pounded in the cork, the third stuck on a label, the fourth put a seal on the cork, and the fifth put the bottle in the case box. Needless to say, this after-school crew was not the solution for bottling our salad dressing. We also traveled to a plant in North Carolina to see a major bottler, who, as it turned out, was interested only in runs of one hundred thousand or more.

We considered taking on a partner, and with that in mind we approached the Bigelow Tea Company in neighboring Norwalk. But they were unenthusiastic about our potential and turned us down.

"You guys are small potatoes," the plant manager told us.

I ran into him years later. By then we were bigger than they were. "Turned out we were king-size Idahos," I said.

I made an appointment with a mayonnaise bottler in the Bushwick section of Brooklyn, the Umbria Company. When I arrived, I was frisked and escorted to a crowded office where, through the thick haze of cigar smoke, I was faced with a group of five men who wore bright neckties and sported diamond rings on their pinkies.

The guy behind the desk, who had hands the size of catcher's mitts, did the talking.

"So, kid, you're into salad dressing with this Newman actor and you're looking to get it bottled, right? Okay. You're usin' olive oil? Good. That's where we come in. In fact, that's where we are. Take a look at that glass case over there . . . no, not the one with the guns, the one with the Umbria olive oil. That's us—we got olive oil by the balls. You use our olive oil, we bottle your dressing, you'll have dressing by the balls. Show him the line, Sal."

Sal, who was the size of an NBA center gone to seed, stood up and led me through a door that opened into an area where an assembly line was filling bottles of mayonnaise. I was expecting a scrubbed Hellmann's-esque scene with white-robed, hair-netted workers tending rows of antiseptically serviced jars; instead, I saw a line of disheveled people who looked like they had been kicked out of a homeless shelter. Sal was probably short for Salmonella.

"Well, kid," said the godfather behind the desk, "we'll spring for the olive oil and we split fifty-fifty, but we got to go with the Umbria name, not this—what'd you call it?"

"Newman's Own."

"No, you ain't."

"I'll let you know."

"What's to know? We got a deal."

"I've got to talk to Newman."

"Why?"

"He's my partner."

"Call him up."

"Right. I've got his number in the car. I'll be right back."

There are still track marks from my car's tires, bearing indelible testimony to my frightened foot on the gas pedal.

I THINK I would have scuttled the salad-dressing adventure by now if it hadn't been for Paul's insistence. Scarcely a day passed that he didn't call from some unlikely place to discuss a newly discovered source for ingredients—the perfect olive oil, the perfect red wine vinegar, the perfect mustard, and so on—which he constantly sought. He phoned me from racetracks in between races, from mobile dressing rooms on location while shooting *Absence of Malice* in Florida with Sally Field, from airports on his way to make speeches on behalf of the nuclear freeze movement, and even, on one occasion, from where he was making a coffee commercial with a Japanese film crew, a background of cacophonous Nipponese chatter making it difficult for me to hear him.

PAUL HAD ALWAYS been perverse about complacency. It was his theory that he had to keep things off-balance or it's *finito*. That's why he took up racing cars when everyone said, "Not when you're forty-seven years old. You out of your mind?" It took him ten years to learn the ropes but doggedness got him there, an old guy winning four national titles. That perversity also accounted for many of his risky movie roles, going where he hadn't been before, running the risk of falling on his face. Running the same risk with the salad dressing. A movie guy and his writer buddy going hard against the odds. Like Butch and Sundance jumping off a cliff into a business-and-marketing canyon—the fall will get us if the sharks in the supermarkets don't. It was a lunatic thing, like a bumblebee or a helicopter. There's no reason for it to fly, but then again, there were the Wright brothers.

It occurred to me that he was Tom Sawyer and I was painting an endless fence.

*P*aul and I are ordering pastrami sandwiches at Gold's Delicatessen on the Post Road in Connecticut. Bearded, well-padded Julius Gold is preparing the sandwiches that we're about to take on the boat with us.

"Julius," Paul says, "if I bottle up my salad dressing would you sell it here?"

"Of course," Julius said in his basso profundo. "I would display it right here next to the counter. When will you have it?"

"As soon as we can find a bottler. Do you happen to know of one?"

"No, but a food broker could help you. I have a customer who's with a small outfit, Northeast Brokerage. I'll give you his phone number."

The broker was a short, compact, natty man named David Kalman, who had the hearty handshake and optimistic smile of a veteran salesman. Don't worry, he said, no problem, the two words he applied to all concerns.

I contacted a man I knew who had been chief executive at General Electric and a top banana at both RJR Nabisco and Standard Brands. I asked him what he thought of our chances with our dressing in the marketplace. "Well," he said, "you're up against Kraft, which has fifteen facings, and you're up against Wishbone and half a dozen other name brands, so I don't think you have a prayer. You'd be better

All's well that ends well for rookie entrepreneurs.

off selling it by mail order. Put a little ad in the back of *The New Yorker*, for example, announcing Paul Newman is making his own salad dressing—people will send you their checks and you can send them a bottle by mail."

After several fits and starts, David finally located a bottler named Andy Crowley, who was exactly the kind of bottler we were seeking; Crowley ran Ken's, a small bottling operation outside Boston that made dressing for Ken's Steakhouse, a modest Boston restaurant.

It is now 1982 and Paul was in Boston filming *The Verdict* when I reached him in his trailer to tell him the good news.

"Okay, let's go full out with it."

"There's a problem—they say we have to have a twelve-month shelf life, but since we're all-natural and don't have preservatives they say it won't fly. They say we can eliminate artificial color and gum, but that we have to compromise and use some EDTA."

"What's that?"

"A chemical with a killer name—I'll spell it for you if you've got a pencil: ethylenediaminetetraacetic acid. With a name like that you can see what we're up against. They say it's the only thing that binds the iron and copper that occur in water. If not bound the iron and copper will be disastrous on the oil. I guess we have to use it."

"No, damnit, no! We're all-natural. No go!"

"But, Paul, it's the only way—"

"Hotch, listen, it's amazing what a 'no' can do. Tell 'em no and see what happens."

"It's never been done."

"Tell 'em no."

"Paul, listen to me—I can tell the bottler and his chemist no, but who's going to make all those nasty spoilers bug off and not contaminate our dressing? So let's find a substitute for 'all-natural.'"

"You are weaseling! We can't weasel! No chemicals means NO chemicals!"

"It also means NO bottles on any store's shelf."

"So you want to cave in, that it?"

"I want to be realistic."

"No, you want to cave in."

"I don't see that a little sprinkle of EDTA is all that important."

"You don't, huh? Well, I'll take over. You can step aside."

"Fine! This is a lost cause anyway."

We hung up. He was seething and I was seething. I'm a writer! I shouted to the window. The hell with salad dressing! Let him find out for himself! I paced around the room, pausing occasionally to hurl zingers at Paul. It didn't last very long. The pacing slowed, the zingers subsided, and I collapsed on the sofa feeling terrible.

I went over to the telephone, trying to think of what to say when it rang.

"Hotchnik, tell you what—"

"Just about to call you, Paul. You're right, we'll tell them no EDTA and see what happens after they test our dressing."

"Keep me posted."

The president and vice president had had their first disagreement, but it had been amicably resolved without the intervention of the board of directors.

The Newman's Own all-natural dressing went to the Ken's chemists without benefit of EDTA or any other preservative. The result was another triumph for Lady Luck and her entourage. Conclusion: the shelf life of Paul's dressing was projected beyond that of the other brands and, as a bonus, the Newman's Own, unlike all the others, did not have to be refrigerated after it was opened. The explanation for these phenomena was simple: the mustard seed. Paul's formula called for crushed mustard seeds. In the long history of bottled dressings no one had ever used mustard seeds, which, when crushed, emitted a natural gum that thoroughly preserved the contents.

Paul didn't seem a bit surprised at the outcome. "It's only the beginning," he said, "wait till they meet our spaghetti sauce."

"Our spaghetti sauce? What spaghetti sauce?"

"Yep, that's gonna be our next product."

WHEN PAUL CAME back to Westport after finishing *The Verdict*, his demeanor had become a bit more serious. I attributed it to his immersion in his role, that of an alcoholic, down-on-his-luck lawyer. His hair was longer and his speech had a touch of an accent and seemed slower, even a bit halting. We were having lunch at Mario's and for the first time within memory he ordered spaghetti Bolognese instead of his routine hamburger.

"What's this about spaghetti sauce?"

"I came in late at night from Boston. Joanne was in New York. The house was deserted. I was starving. Fridge empty. Cupboard empty except for one jar of spaghetti sauce and a packet of spaghetti. Boiled water for the spaghetti, poured the sauce in a pan—it oozed out like red crankcase oil. Poured sauce on spaghetti, first mouthful— spit it out in the sink. You ever try spaghetti sauce from a jar? Don't. Nothing in it. No veggies, meat, cheese—nada."

"You're supposed to add stuff to it."

"How about we add the stuff right in the jar?"

"All right. But slow down. We haven't produced a bottle of salad dressing yet and we're down to twenty thousand dollars in our kitty."

"Well, that's our priority but we've got to be thinking ahead. Now if we're going to be taken seriously as a couple of food mavens . . . this is what I wrote coming down here from Boston. My business résumé. It's your turn."

"What are you talking about? What business résumé?"

"Here, read this." He handed me a couple of handwritten pages. "You write yours and I'll send them to Warren Cowan, my movie publicist, to send them out."

My father had a sporting goods store in Cleveland (we lived in suburban Shaker Heights) and I used to work there on Saturdays, so I guess from early on I lived in a business atmosphere. As a boy I earned money with the usual boy things—a paper route, cleaning golf balls at a driving range, and when I was at Yale for the year I studied for a master's degree in speech (I was running out of my GI Bill funds), I sold the Encyclopedia Britannica door-to-door—I once earned nine hundred dollars in ten days. I had another door-to-door employment as a Fuller Brush salesman. But my *pièce de résistance* was the laundry-and-beer business I started when I was at Kenyon College in Gambier, Ohio. The laundry company used to come to the dorms, going from room to room to pick up individual laundry, but I made a deal with the company for a much lower rate if they picked up the laundry at one site in the town. I rented an abandoned storefront in a partially developed part of Gambier, on a dirt road of sorts there, fixed it up and advertised in the school paper that my laundry service would serve free beer to any customer bringing in his laundry. I had figured out the cost of a keg of beer, plus rent and the laundry's charges, against what I charged for the laundry, and the way it turned out I did a thriving business, pocketing seventy, eighty dollars a week. This was 1948, so that's like five hundred bucks a week today. I finally sold the business in my senior year to a friend of mine and as luck would have it, a month or so later one of the customers who had over-imbibed the free beer put on a boxing glove, staggered out into the street, and started to masturbate a horse that was tied up there. The authorities shut down the business, busting the whole shop.

Those days at Kenyon were the happiest of my life. I joined the student drama society and acted in a variety of plays even though I was terrorized by the emotional requirements of being an actor—acting is like letting your pants down in public, you're exposed—but I enjoyed the overall stage experience. I also enjoyed playing on the football team until I did a really dumb thing and shot myself in the foot. There had been a serious rumble in a local bar between some of us footballers and a group of townies. The police broke up the fracas and rounded up all the miscreants, but somehow I was able to wander off without being nabbed. Later that night, however, when I went to the police station to give the quarterback his car keys, one of the cops noticed my scruffed knuckles, and he tossed me into the slammer with the rest. As a result, I got kicked off the football team.

Although my laundry-and-beer business success was a feather in my cap, I preferred to keep it as an isolated business triumph, so that when my father died in 1950 and my mother asked me to return to Shaker Heights and take over the business, I did so with a heavy heart. I was acting with a summer stock company in Woodstock, Illinois, and had appeared in seventeen different productions. I married one of the actresses, Jacqueline Witte, who soon became pregnant. I was pretty well set on an acting career but I felt I had to respect my mother's request to return and help run the store. There was irony in this, in that my father, a brilliant, erudite man with a marvelous, whimsical sense of humor, when he was seventeen had been the youngest reporter ever hired by the *Cleveland Press* but he had to give up that career to go into the family business, just as now I had to leave off being an actor to take over the business. I think my father always thought of me as pretty much of a lightweight. He treated me like he was disappointed in me—he had every right to be. It has been one of the great agonies of my life that he never knew how I turned out. I wanted desperately to show him that somehow, somewhere along the line I could cut the mustard. But I never got a chance. I had such respect for him, as a man, for his integrity. In the Depression, he was able to get $200,000 worth of consignment goods from Spalding and Rawlings because his reputation for paying, his honesty, was so impeccable. He had so many admirable qualities: ethical, moral, funny. But he was distant, beyond embrace.

When my brother and I went into the war—I was a radio operator—my father wrote us every single day, each of us. Every day for three years, he sent us a letter. If you go back and look at the letters, they were distant. There was no familial sense to them. But there was an obligation to somehow remind us that there was somebody back home that was thinking about us.

After I read his résumé, I said, "What will this do for Newman's Own?"

"Hotch," he said patiently, "we're about to sell salad dressing and this will set up our credentials so we're not just an actor and a writer. Now it's your turn."

"My turn at what? I have even less credentials than you."

"You're always so damned negative! You think we're going to make it or not?"

"Sure we are! We're gonna walk on the moon."

"Then write a goddamn résumé."

"Sometimes, Newman," I said testily, "your paranoia clouds your vision."

This résumé is all I could scrape off the bottom of my barrel to send to Warren Cowan along with Paul's:

I was involved in a variety of boyhood money-making endeavors—a paper route, peddling Christmas trees door-to-door, selling tickets on the telephone to the Gas and Electric Workers' annual barbecue, and I had one meaningful entrepreneurial experience. This was during the depths of the Depression, when nobody in my family had a job.

It was summer and it was very hot, and one day I asked my mother if she'd make me a pot of lemonade to sell. I was ten. Lawn Avenue, where we lived, was just a block away from Kingshighway Boulevard, which was nothing but one empty lot after another. No hot-dog stands or ice-cream shops or used-car places, just miles and miles of empty lots. But I had noticed that there was a great deal of traffic along Kingshighway that fed into Route 67, which was the main highway to the south, to Poplar Bluff and places like Arkansas. I figured people driving along there in the heat must have been very thirsty.

I was right. I printed a sign—FRESH LEMONADE 5¢—and sat with my pot at the curb in front of a vacant lot. In twenty minutes I was sold out. Now I had enough money to buy a lot of lemons and sugar, and we made gallons of lemonade that went as fast as the first little batch. By now, I had two neighborhood buddies, Jason Tindell and

Ernie Rich, helping out, and we were selling lemonade at five cents a drink just as fast as we could pour it. The cars would stop along the curb and we'd bring them their lemonade and they'd pay us through the window. That's when the Nehi soda man stopped. He saw all these cars buying lemonade. He was starving for business as much as the next guy, so he told me if I could put up a stand with a roof he could furnish me with a Nehi icebox and ice and all the flavors of Nehi soda.

Naturally to build a stand I needed wood and nails and all that, but there wasn't any building going on in the neighborhood (where I could "borrow" what I needed) because if you're a builder and you can't rent or sell what you've got, why build more? But I mounted my old Century bike, which was really Silver and I was the Lone Ranger, and rode all over until I found a place where someone was building a garage. That night, I got Jason and Ernie and we snuck over there and "borrowed" all the materials for the stand, which we then built and painted (Ernie's father was a paint salesman) in two days. The Nehi man brought the icebox and six cases of Nehi soda, which came in long thin bottles with a picture of a lady's leg wearing a garter on every bottle. The Nehi man also brought a big tin sign to put on top of the stand that had "Nehi" all around it, and in a white place in the middle it said in black letters, AARON'S ICE COLD POP. That sign made a big impression on me. I felt like I was on Broadway or on the Tivoli movie marquee.

In no time at all, I had four Nehi iceboxes, hot dogs, and popcorn from a machine I bought for two dollars from a movie house on Chippewa that had gone broke. I also had eight kids on the block working for me and we were open nights. I was able to be open nights because that part of St. Louis still had gas lamps, and every night around six Enrico, a plump little Italian man, would go by with his lamplighter pole over his shoulder, lighting the lamps on Kingshighway. He would always stop and have a soda, and one day I said, "Enrico, I wish you were lighting a lamp here, because people can't see us once it gets dark." Enrico knew all the kids who were working for me, because he had been lighting lamps up and down their streets from before they were born, so he said, with this big, wonderful mustache smile he had, "Why not?" The next day, he came by in the afternoon pushing a handcart on which he had the top parts of two old lampposts. We hung them on the front corners of the stand, and every night after that when Enrico went by, he lighted our two lamps. Of course, from then on he got all his sodas free.

One other thing I did. I practiced drawing the Nehi leg until I was really good at it. Ernie got a can of orange paint from his father, and one day we roped off half the street in front of the stand and I painted a huge Nehi leg on the street with an arrow pointing our way. Did we do business! I gave some profits to my mother to pay all the bills, and saved some money in my secret box. The Nehi man said I was the best customer he had.

But one day a Mr. A. W. Brown showed up and it all ended. He explained very nicely that he had been watching the business we did and had bought the lot to put up a root-beer stand and miniature golf course. He offered me a job either in the root-beer stand or the golf course, but no matter how nice he was, it was like Little Caesar coming in and telling me to get out of his territory. All the kids who had been working for me were standing in a circle around us and they were all looking at me, expecting me to *do* something.

A. W. Brown's workmen started in the very next day, and it only took them about ten minutes to tear down our stand and cart away the pieces. Enrico came for the lamplights. In about a week's time the root-beer stand was open, with A. W. Brown's name on it, and the miniature golf a week after that. People didn't have money to eat, but they had money for miniature golf.

I RECEIVED A call from Warren Cowan, an affable veteran of the Hollywood public relations wars. "Tell me something, Hotch," Warren said, "what am I supposed to do with these two . . . two . . . documents?"

"Paul thinks they will give us some standing in the business world."

"He wants me to send these . . . these . . . like, to the business section of *The New York Times*?"

I didn't answer.

"A laundry-and-beer business and a soda-pop stand?"

I cringed. "Tell you what, Warren—how about filing them away until we get a little further down the line?"

I heard his sigh of relief. "Just what I was going to suggest," he said.

We're having a frolicsome afternoon in Paul's barn with a good friend, Steve Calhoun, who ranks high on the list of professional photographers, right up there with Richard Avedon and Irving Penn. Indulging our zany impulses, Paul and I have conjured up costumes that we imagine present us in our best food-mogul guise. Paul has pretty much re-created his Butch Cassidy look and I have assembled a costume that blends a Marx brother with one of the Three Stooges and Buster Keaton.

We are staging this photo shoot in the barn to generate images that can be used for publicity—the two of us in various stages of eating salad with competitors' dressings and with our own, enacting our preparation of the dressing, highlighting the moment we "discover" our dressing—Steve's busy camera catching us in action.

Joanne comes in to watch and is vastly amused by our antics. She has overcome her initial skepticism and is now enjoying our Newman's Own enterprise. In fact, later that afternoon, along with her daughters and Caroline the housekeeper, Joanne is going to help us reenact a bowdlerized version of our Christmas distribution of the bottled dressing.

We have resorted to these photo sessions because, as I have said, we didn't have the resources to underwrite advertising and because Paul decided that advertising his dressing was "tacky." How he rationalized that these zany publicity photos would be less tacky than

Out of the basement and into the sunlight of success.

advertising was never revealed, but getting them published in newspapers and magazines would be free publicity for a company whose capital was quickly diminishing.

I am by no means an actor, but performing these bits with Paul before Steve's camera gave me an unexpected insight into what emanates from Paul when he's acting, even at this impromptu level. It is an enveloping quality, a magnetism that pulled me into his orbit, bonding the two of us. I could now better understand what made his performances with Robert Redford and Patricia Neal, Elizabeth Taylor and Tom Cruise so compelling.

NOW THAT KEN'S was ready to fill our first batch of bottles, it was necessary to prepare them for distribution. We were *really* in business, but we were determined that it not turn into *serious* business. We devised a mock-Napoleonic "N" with a laurel wreath around it for the neck of the bottle. On the label we poked fun at the corny hype on our competitors' bottles with *Nomen Vide Optima Expecta* ("See the Name, Expect the Best")—finally I got some use out of my three years of high-school Latin. We also used the words "Tutto Naturale," and in place of copyright notice, Paul suggested "Appellation Newman Contrôlée." As a spoof of businesses that tout their ancestry, we had great fun with the slogan: "Fine Foods Since February." For the back of the bottle, we composed the first of the legends that would eventually appear on all our products.

——————— ✦ ✦ ✦ ———————

Why? Why market this all-natural, no-nonsense, kick-in-the-derrière dressing? In a word—the neighbors. For years, at Christmas, old pal Hotchner and I bottled this concoction for friends. The acclaim was deafening, the repeat orders staggering. This year, they chained us to the furnace until we brewed 30 gallons—a prisoner of my own excellence. Enough! I said. Let's go public! I'm out of the basement and onto the shelf!—*P. Loquesto Newman*

We are meeting with Stew Leonard, whose name adorns a giant supermarket in nearby Norwalk. We are seeking marketing advice from Stew, who is a phenomenal promoter of specialty foods.

"Well, gents, I'll speak straight to you," Stew says, smiling the cherub smile that appears on all his shopping bags along with Elsie the Cow. "All my attempts to sell celebrity products here have fizzled—Roger Staubach's peanut butter, Graziano's spaghetti sauce— fizzled because they weren't anything special. I've tasted your dressing. It's darned good and you've got a good start, Paul. You'll sell the first bottle because your face is on the label."

"Whoa!" Paul says. "My face is on the *label*?"

"Naturally. How you gonna get their attention? You said you weren't going to advertise, so how will the customer know it's you?"

"It'll say Newman's Own."

"For all they know, that could be Seymour Newman from Newark, New Jersey. Take it from me, you will not be able to sell bottle one unless your face is on the label, that's for sure."

"My face on a bottle of salad dressing? Not a chance in hell."

"Tell you what, Paul. Get a good label with you looking right at the shopper, and I'll kick off your sales with a big promotion in my store."

.   .   .

Stew Leonard sold ten thousand bottles in two weeks.

"HE'S RIGHT," I SAID as we headed back to Westport.

"What do you mean, he's right?"

"That it could be Seymour Newman."

"Put my face on the windshield of a Mercedes-Benz or a Volvo maybe . . . but salad dressing?"

"Why don't we bag the whole thing? It isn't as if we *have* to go into the salad-dressing business."

"So that's the solution? Give up?"

"We agreed if it got to the point where we weren't having fun being salad-dressing moguls—"

"Let's shut up and think, okay?"

We stopped at the Westport tackle shop and bought a dozen worms before heading to the marina where *Caca IV* was berthed. Paul started the engine and I freed us from the mooring post. We anchored at buoy 13, baited a couple of rods, cast them, and put them in holders with bobbers on the lines. We floated along for a while, glumly watching the non-bobbing bobbers. I suggested that we should rethink this entire venture—maybe it was an ill-conceived, impetuous mistake. The bobber dipped and Paul reeled in a hermit crab.

"You know, there could be a kind of justice here, Hotchnik. I go on television all the time to hustle my films. TV gets me and my time for free, and the film gets exposure for free—mutual and circular exploitation, so to speak. Now then, if we were to go to the lowest of the low road and plaster my face on a bottle of oil-and-vinegar dressing just to line our pockets, it would stink. But to go the low road to get to the high road—shameless exploitation for charity, for the common good—now there's an idea worth the hustle, a reciprocal trade agreement."

"You mean give all the profits away?"

"There probably won't be any. You heard Stew—what happened to Graziano's spaghetti sauce."

"But Stew said he'd promote ours."

"Let's say it does make a few bucks. You'll be a philanthropist. Doesn't that appeal to you?"

"What appeals to me is the day I see that bottle of Newman's Own right up there on the shelf alongside Wishbone. If we make a couple of bucks and I give it away, so be it."

"Exactly—so be it. Racing buddy of mine—Sam Posey—his wife, Ellen, is an artist. I'll ask her to draw me for the label and there I'll be, the star of a bottle of oil-and-vinegar dressing."

STEW LEONARD'S PROMOTION was a wonderful baptism for our newborn bottle. He put a mound of iceberg lettuce next to rows of Newman's Own dressing with this sign: BUY TWO JARS, GET A FREE HEAD OF LETTUCE. In two weeks ten thousand bottles were sold and Ken's had to put extra shifts on their production line. Paul made the mistake of visiting Stew's market, causing gridlock. We were in business but we didn't have an office, a bookkeeper, or any employees, not even a telephone. For starters, our lawyer's bookkeeper helped set up our books, and we rented a two-room office across the hall from his office, which was located above a bank on the Post Road in Westport. Only ten thousand dollars remained in our treasury after paying for labels, bottles, and all that, so instead of buying office furniture, Paul decided that since it was September and he was closing his swimming pool, he would simply furnish the office with his pool furniture, even to the extent of keeping a beach umbrella over our shared desk (his picnic table). Paul's Ping-Pong table became our conference table, but the only conferences we held were when we played Ping-Pong. Paul wrote our scores on the low ceiling, but when his losses mounted significantly he had the ceiling painted. On the wall beside our desk we put up a graph that would chart our sales from September, when we first started, to January.

We also posted a few signs on the walls of our new office to create the proper atmosphere for our renegade business:

JUST WHEN THINGS LOOK DARKEST
THEY GO BLACK.

IT IS USELESS TO PUT ON THE BRAKES
WHEN YOU ARE UPSIDE DOWN.

YOU CAN GET STRAIGHT A'S IN MARKETING
AND STILL FLUNK ORDINARY LIFE.

It was September 1982, and we decided that there had been enough foreplay—it was time to get into the actual act. With our meager capital, we couldn't possibly advertise, so Paul decided to make our worldly launch a really tacky but attention-getting debut. In keeping with our renegade philosophy, we rejected such glitzy New York City venues as the Four Seasons and "21" in favor of Hanratty's, a joint Paul liked, a grungy bar and grill located at Ninetieth and Second Avenue, an inaccessible, unfashionable neighborhood. David Kalman invited the head buyers for the big supermarkets, and we hired a freelance publicist to send invitations to the newspapers, television stations, wire services, magazines—the entire media kit and caboodle. We asked Gene Shalit, who had often interviewed Paul about his movies on the *Today* show, to join us for the occasion. To highlight our dressing, Hanratty's would prepare a variety of salads, all using Newman's Own, and there would be an open bar with music provided by a three-piece group of dubious musicality.

AS THE HANRATTY'S launch day moved closer, Paul became increasingly nervous about whether the event would have any impact with the media. "I don't want to be stuck in front of those cameras having to answer a barrage of dumb questions. You're the writer—*think* of something, some kind of commotion. We know how bad I am at interviews."

So now we are on my terrace, grilling hot dogs, and I am about to unveil my Hanratty material: salad-dressing lyrics I have written to the music of Gilbert and Sullivan's "I Am the Very Model of a Modern Major-General," plus a love song set to Richard Rodgers' music for "Where or When."

Paul is delighted. "Good going. About time you put your ass in gear. Now I'll tell you what we need—somebody unexpected to sing it. How about Luciano Pavarotti?"

"Pavarotti? Well, he's certainly unexpected but I don't think he'll be available to sing a salad-dressing aria."

"There you go—a negative foot-dragger." He picked up the phone and asked his assistant to find out where he could reach Signor Pavarotti.

We had just finished our hot dogs when Paul got word of where Pavarotti was staying in San Francisco. Paul dialed the number and a sleepy "*Pronto*" responded on the speakerphone.

"Is this Luciano Pavarotti?" Paul asked.

"*Sì.*"

"This is Paul Newman calling."

"Who?"

"Paul Newman."

"The actor?"

"*Sì.* I'm introducing my salad dressing at an event next Tuesday and there's a song that I thought you might get a kick out of."

"You are Paul Newman the actor? The Butch person?"

"It's just a fun event, nothing serious."

"*Sì, sì*, but I am *dispiace*. I cannot because next Tuesday I sing *Pagliacci* with the San Francisco Opera."

"Oh . . . well . . . all right. Thanks anyway. Just thought I'd give it a try."

"*Ciao.*"

There was a hang-up click on the speakerphone.

"Now, then," Paul said, "let's try Plácido Domingo."

He picked up the phone but I pushed the disconnect. "Paul, you're not being practical." He put the phone down. "The event is next Tuesday. There is only one person who is able to sing the song."

"Who?"

"You."

"Me? I have a voice like an ice pick."

"I happen to know you sang 'Love and Marriage' in the musical of *Our Town*, for a TV special with Frank Sinatra."

"That was in a television studio, not in front of a slew of cameras and news people."

"You wanted the unexpected, didn't you?"

"Yeah, but this is a lousy way to kill off the little bit that's left of my career."

I WENT TO see Joanne in the Newmans' apartment in the Carlyle and told her about the Hanratty's event.

"Paul is going to sing?"

"Yep."

"Are you sure?"

"And so are you."

"And so am I what?"

"Going to sing. It's a salad-dressing love song set to Richard Rodgers' music for 'Where or When.' "

"You're having press people?"

"TV cameras. The works."

"And I croon a love song to a salad dressing?"

"It's a great Rodgers melody."

"I know the song."

"That's swell!"

"But with the original words."

"You can't leave Paul up there all alone."

"Up where?"

"We've built a little stage."

"Where?"

"Hanratty's Bar and Grill."

"And you two think you're going to make a go of that salad dressing?"

"Sure—if you and Paul will sing."

Joanne took a long breath and stared at me with narrowed eyes.

"Hotch, to all your other deficiencies I will now add devious."

"Thanks, Joanne. I appreciate the compliment."

HANRATTY'S WAS FILLED to overflowing: three camera crews, reporters from all the New York papers and the Associated Press, movie people, food critics, and the CEOs of several supermarket chains. Paul kept a very steady Gilbert and Sullivan beat, with his backup chorus of three legal aids from Nevas's law office.

To the tune of "I Am the Very Model of a Modern Major-General"

I've tasted all the dressings on the shelves at food emporiums,
And most of them taste like they should be served in vomitoriums.
I'm very well acquainted too with dressings that you mix at home,
And thrust upon the visiting and unsuspecting gastronome.
But as for me I much prefer to eat my salad in the sack,
And that is why in Newman's Own you'll find an aphrodisiac.

Chorus
And that is why in Newman's Own
You'll find an aphrodisiac . . .

Which brings me to the subject of this bottle's true ingredients,
That I will now reveal to you with candor and expedience.

In short, when you have tasted it, you'll know just what you're get-ett-
ing,
Feel free to strip and lurch about with naughty piroue-ett-ing.

Chorus
In short, when you have tasted it, you'll know just what you're get-ett-
ing,
Feel free to strip and lurch about with naughty piroue-ett-ing.

To find the proper olive oil we searched through several continents,
To find the one that had the most extraordinary redolence,
From sunny Spain to Portugal and then on to Transylvania,
How the hell was I to know we'd find the stuff in Pennsylvania?

The clever spices we have added are a well-kept mystery,
And everything is natural to ward off flu and dysent'ry!
So now I have explained to you with all my cogent reasonings,
Why I hope that I am known as the man for all good seasonings!

Joanne got into the spirit of things with a campy rendition of
my butchery of Rodgers and Hart.

Some couples frolic in the nude,
Doing things rather lewd.
But for us,
Our aptitude
Was sharing sexy food.
The mem'ry of the meals we ate,
Still makes me salivate,
Tasting things
From off your fork—
Onion rings
On poached pork—
Listen how my stomach sings!

Chorus

It seems we sat and ate like this before,
The chopped chicken liver in the pastry shell,
I remember that the smell was swell.
The lox we're eating is the lox we ate,
The bagels and cream cheese really sealed our fate,
You were a virgin and I was celibate.
But when the salad course came to you,
Then you jumped up and said, "We're through!"
But now, my darling, we have Newman's Own
To sprinkle on the salad of our love
Forever more.

Gene Shalit then delivered this monologue:

Over the years, I have been prepared for great things from Paul
Newman, but a prepared salad dressing was not among them. I was
naturally on my guard. Caution was called for, so I went back and
checked out my reviews of his movies. *Butch Cassidy* was good, and so
was *The Sting* . . . but I really felt safe when I noticed that I was one
of the few people in America who admired *Quintet*. In fact, I was
one of the few people in America who saw *Quintet*. So I figured it was
safe to try a spoonful. I discovered that its unusual flavor comes from a
most unusual oil—Mobil One. The mixture was blended with exotic
spices in his Datsun crankcase. In fact, to test it, Paul first used it in his
Datsun 280ZX, which is how he won at Brainerd, Minnesota, this year.
They needed a name. A marketing expert was called in—a woman it so
happened—and she suggested "Paul Newman's Undressing." Joanne
dismissed her. When Sophia Loren rang me up the other day, I told her
that "Paul Newman is putting out a salad dressing." Sophia said, "What
came after 'Paul Newman is putting out'?"

A cynic told me that to get to the truth of this project, you need
only look at the names of some of Paul's movies: *The Hustler*, *Pocket
Money*, and *The Outrage*. I countered with *Sometimes a Great Notion*.

This is going to be a very special year for Paul: the appearance of Newman's Own here in September . . . and the release in December of *The Verdict*, an exceptional film in which he gives an extraordinary performance. Clearly, these are Paul Newman's salad days.

NOW THAT HE had compromised his reputation by putting his face on the salad dressing, Paul was resigned—no, invigorated by the spontaneous success of what had started as a lighthearted lark, a spoof, a loser's gamble. With the engine cranked and turned over, Paul was eager to get behind the wheel and qualify it for a do-or-die run against the big boys. He and I got together with Steve Calhoun to devise a couple of posters that could be exhibited in stores around the country: Paul as a gourmet chef, Paul juggling the ingredients of a tossed salad.

In addition to the posters, the notoriety of Newman's Own was being further hyped by a spate of cartoons, like this one, which appeared in *The New Yorker*:

"Blue-cheese, Thousand Island, or Paul Newman?"

*O*ur nirvana was suddenly overcast by a lawsuit that landed Paul and me in the superior court in Bridgeport, Connecticut, superior in name only, with Judge Howard F. Zoarski presiding. A few years back, when Paul was directing *Gamma Rays*, he had referred to Bridgeport in a press interview as "a depressing little town, the armpit of New England," and now in its current edition *The Bridgeport Post* is reminding its readers of that derogatory slam. Not a pretty remark for the panel of six Bridgeport jurors to be reading at the start of our trial.

The plaintiff in this action is Julius Gold, that delicatessen owner who, while slicing pastrami for our sandwiches, had given us the name of one of his customers who was a food broker. Now Paul, me, Newman's Own, and the broker, David Kalman, are all being sued by Julius, who claims that he was instrumental in the success of our business and is seeking a certain amount of stock for his efforts.

Even though we're an S corporation with Paul as the sole stockholder, Julius is persisting in his quest for ownership so that, as he says, "I can give money to *my* charities." Paul and I were co-owners of the business, he had 75 percent to my 25 percent, but when we decided to give all profits after taxes to charity, issuing stock became moot.

The trial is a media circus with television and press all over the courthouse steps. It is a lovely June day, and the last place we want to be is in this small, dingy, moldy courtroom having to defend a frivolous lawsuit brought by a man who had absolutely nothing to do with the formation of Newman's Own other than to suggest a possible food broker.

When Julius first surfaced with his demand for compensation, Paul and I were puzzled.

"Has Julius ever talked to you about Newman's Own?" Paul asked.

"No, how about you?"

"Nope. I was in the deli one time for a loaf of rye and he asked me when he'd be getting the dressing in order to sell it in the store. That's it. What's this all about?"

"I guess he wants to get in on a good thing."

"Is he broke?"

"I don't think so. I think he wants to rub elbows with you and be more than a delicatesseneer. He has pretensions. I think he plays the bassoon."

"Well he better learn to play '*Dixie*' because that's where he'll be headed."

THE TRIAL HAS been preceded by months of time-consuming costly motions and depositions—money that could have gone to charities instead of lawyers—but the rotund, bearded Julius is basking in the attention he is getting, although now on cross-examination, he is not helping his cause.

"Mr. Gold, did you have anything to do with the concoction of the salad dressing?"

"No."

"Did you participate in the initial stages of mixing the salad dressing, bottling it, etcetera?"

"No."

"Did you have anything to do with writing the legend on the label?"

The defendants with their trial attorney, Patrick Ryan, his assistant, Stew Leonard (front left), and attorney Leo Nevas.

"No."

"Did you have anything to do with selling the products or promoting the products in any way?"

"Well, I sold the dressing in my delicatessen, and many of my ideas contributed to the marketing and success of the product."

Of course Julius had nothing to do with us other than to give us Kalman's name, but he spent several days on the witness stand pontificating about himself and his supposed contributions. Now, when pressed on cross-examination, he couldn't particularize those contributions.

Afterward, he basked in the glory of being interviewed on the courthouse steps by the daily phalanx of reporters, hungry for coverage of this seismographic event, which the press called "The Salad War." "I no longer stock Newman's Own in my delicatessen," he grandly told the reporters.

My turn on the witness stand was prolonged by nitpicking questions from Gold's lawyer, Richard Albrecht, who was desperately trying to build a case. We did have one exchange that got the courtroom laughing.

Albrecht: "Besides being CEO of Newman's Own, you are a writer?"

Hotchner: "Yes."

Albrecht: "You have done something on Sophia Loren?"

Hotchner: "No, I never had the opportunity."

Paul was scheduled for the witness stand the following day. On our way to the courthouse that morning, I talked to him about his impending testimony.

"I know you just played a lawyer in *The Verdict*, but keep in mind this is real life here not your movie courtroom. Because of who you are the jury will be impressed if you keep your answers simple and direct, just plain and honest."

Our attorney, Patrick Ryan, handed Paul a bottle of our dressing and asked if Gold had had anything to do with any of its contents, labels, legends, etcetera, which Paul denied. In answering another question about the success of Newman's Own, Paul replied, "It is embarrassing that the salad dressing is now outgrossing my films in profits."

Ryan turned Paul over to Albrecht for cross-examination, and the questions went from general to personal. I could tell that Paul was getting increasingly irritated, but he was holding his own until Albrecht, desperately goading him, asked, "Isn't it true, Mr. Newman, that despite what you have told the court, a substantial part of Newman's Own profits go to a great many people who are not charities?"

Paul was instantly up from the witness chair, brandishing the salad-dressing bottle, starting to charge Albrecht who began to retreat.

"You sonofabitch," Paul shouted, "that's a damned lie! You and Gold are two of a kind!"

Ryan and his assistant, quickly up from their table, grabbed Paul by his arms to restrain him. This caused the salad-dressing bottle to slip from his grasp and fall to the floor, shattering and spilling a pool of its oil-and-vinegar contents in front of the witness chair, some of it splashing on Albrecht's shoes.

Judge Zoarski used his gavel for the first time. Bang, bang, bang! "The court will come to order." Bang, bang, bang! "All parties will now sit down." Bang, bang, bang! "The clerk is now instructed to deal with the pool of liquid on the floor. The jury will please disregard Mr. Albrecht's question and Mr. Newman's response."

When Paul returned to his seat, he whispered to me, "What'd you think?"

"Your performance was better in *The Verdict*."

Afterward, on the courthouse steps, surrounded by media, in a neat alliteration Paul called Gold's attorney arrogant, abusive, and abrasive.

The trial lugubriously droned on, devouring almost all of the lovely June weather, before finally going to the jury, which consisted of a Bridgeport University professor plus five jurors in their twenties. After several hours of anxious waiting, it was revealed that when the trial ended, the clerk had accidentally brought the pretrial depositions of the principals into the jury room. Depositions are not admissible as evidence and not to be read by the jury (two jurors had read them). As a result, the judge had no choice but to declare a mistrial, which meant going through this ordeal all over again. Julius immediately announced, "As a matter of principle, I will not walk away from this cause." It also assured Julius of another long round of getting his name and picture in the newspaper and on the evening television news, linked to Paul Newman, and every day, after the court adjourned, he could exercise his verbosity in front of the press.

The retrial didn't get back on the docket until the following year. It was just as long and tedious and pointless, but this time the jury room was not contaminated with depositions and the verdict was swift and unanimous, finding for us on all counts.

*P*aul and I are in our office sitting at our shared desk (his poolside picnic table) with the big beach umbrella overhead and on the table, the two brass nameplates that Paul had made for us: A. E. Hotchner, Lifeguard on Duty, and P. L. Newman, Assistant Lifeguard on Duty. We are sharing a pastrami on rye that came from Gold's competition, Oscar's Deli on Main Street; naturally we never again set foot in Gold's Deli. As far as I know Paul never had more than half a sandwich for lunch—pastrami, meatball sub, or chicken—to preserve his movie-star thinness. "Not vanity," he said, "necessity—the camera lens loads you up."

Whereas the salad dressing was the creation of a couple of merry pranksters, a happy accident, the pasta sauce was a deliberate vendetta, Paul's revenge against that offensive bottle of spaghetti sauce that he had found lurking in a corner of his cupboard. He has vowed to rescue the pasta eaters of the world with a Newman's Own sauce that will have whole chunks of vegetables and no preservatives or coloring or any of the other disgusting chemicals that we found in the jars of sauce we sampled from Stop & Shop, jars that without exception were bland, tasteless, sweet, and terrible.

We cooked up a sauce in Paul's kitchen that contained tomato puree, tomato chunks, red and green peppers, celery, mushrooms, olive oil, spices, onion, garlic—all of it fresh, a chunky look to it—and

John LiDestri cutting the ribbon on the new pasta sauce factory, which increased production from sixty bottles a minute to four hundred, seven days a week.

Paul dashed off a legend to put on the bottle, which told it the way it was:

———————— ✦ ✦ ✦ ————————

> Working 12 hour days . . . wrecked . . . hungry . . . arrive home, deserted by wife and children . . . cursing! Scan the cupboard—one package spaghetti—one bottle marinara sauce—run to the kitchen, cook—junk! YUK! Lie down, snooze . . . visions of culinary delights . . . Venetian ancestor tickles my ear, tickle, tickle . . . sauce talk . . . MAMA MIA! Dash to the vegetable patch . . . Yum yum . . . boil water . . . activate spaghetti . . . ditto the sauce . . . slurp, slurp . . . Terrifico! Magnifico! Slurp! Caramba! Bottle the sauce! . . . share with guys on street car . . . ah, me, finally immortal!—*P. Loquesto Newman*

———————————————

WE NOW HAD to invent a name for this sauce, and what we came up with—Newman's Own Industrial Strength All-Natural Venetian-Style Spaghetti Sauce—horrified our brokers. "Industrial strength! They'll think it's for factories—they'll never buy it to put on spaghetti." As usual, we disregarded their "expertise" and told Kalman to concentrate on finding a small company to bottle it.

Eventually he found a small sauce producer in Rochester, New York: Cantisano Foods. Ralph Cantisano was an Italian sauce maker of the old school. He had created Ragú, which became the best-selling sauce in the country, and then sold Ragú to Chesebrough-Pond for a hefty sum and maintained this little plant in Rochester simply as a means of keeping his fine Italian hand in the pasta business.

We are now in our office munching on our demi-pastrami sandwiches, awaiting the arrival of John LiDestri, who is the CEO of Cantisano. A short man with sunny features, he came to the door with an eager smile, but the smile precipitously dropped to his shoes when he saw us under the beach umbrella with this sign on the wall behind us:

LiDestri sat down on a beach chair facing us as we finished our sandwiches. We offered to share our root beer with him, but he declined. "Gentlemen, I'm a blunt person so I'll come right out and tell you I'm rather discouraged by the fact that here you want us to produce this new kind of pasta sauce, invest in very expensive new equipment, but do you have a marketing survey?"

"Nope," Paul said.

"A business plan?"

"Nope."

"A budget?"

"Nope."

"Any organized strategy for its introduction?"

"Nope."

"And you plan to fly into this new venture absolutely blind?"

"Our business," Paul said, "is just part of life's great folly. My philosophy is: Stay loose, men, keep 'em off-balance."

"John," I said, "we are not IBM. You see that motto?" I pointed to the framed sign on another wall that read:

IF WE EVER HAVE A PLAN, WE'RE SCREWED.

"We fly by the seat of our pants and we haven't crashed yet, even though Paul is color-blind."

"So you're asking us to invest our company money and time to gamble on shelf life, which it very likely won't have; on housewives buying chunky sauces, which they probably won't; and on a business that gives all of its capital away in December and in January has to borrow money from the bank to start the new year, a company with no business plan or budget. That's it, isn't it?"

"Yup," I said.

"Don't you think you'd be better off bringing out a traditional sauce and eliminating the risk factors?"

"Nope," Paul said.

BUT LiDESTRI AGREED to go with us. To give an introductory goose to our fledgling spaghetti sauce, we staged a festive media party at Keens Chophouse in Manhattan—not a glamorous spot by any means but suited to the nature of our bizarre company. The media turnout exceeded the Hanratty's introduction of the salad dressing, and with the cameras rolling, Paul and Joanne sang the praises of the spaghetti sauce in songs that I brazenly composed to the music of Frederick Loewe and George Gershwin, both of whom would have been horrified.

To the tune of Loewe's "I've Grown Accustomed to Her Face"

PAUL:

I've tasted sauces from the East
Some made with curdled milk and yeast,
And the spaghetti drenched with grease
That makes you so obese,
It sticks to you,
And tastes like glue,
Those pasta sauces on the shelf,
No self-respecting man would eat.
I have Italian blood that needs a good spaghetti now and then,
Malnutrition almost drove me round the bend—
That's when . . .

There came to me while deep in sleep,
A recipe divine,
A recipe that's mine . . .

To the tune of Gershwin's "I've Got Rhythm"

JOANNE:
It's got onions,
It's got garlic,
It's got basil,
Who could ask for anything more?

It's got olive
Oil and spices,
It's all nat'ral,
True industrial strength galore!

Pride of Venice,
Rome and Pisa,
It'sa sure that
It'll please ya.

Lots of peppers,
Fresh tomatoes,
Cup of sunshine,
Who could ask for anything more?
Who could ask for anything more?

PAUL:
I'm as content as I can be,
That now I have a spaghetti,
Of which my ancestors can be
So justly proud of me—
From Sha-ker Heights,
To Ve-nice nights.

And now Andretti says that he,
Would like to give me the Grand Prix,
For having fin'lly made a sauce that's like he had in Italy,
He then ran a vic'try lap for him and me,
You see . . .

If you will keep on buying them,
It will become a fact,
Newman won't have to act!

JOANNE AND PAUL:
Who could ask for anything more?
Who could ask for anything more?

The Keens kitchen produced a variety of pastas, all anointed with our industrial-strength elixir, on serving platters scattered around the restaurant. The bar flowed freely while scores of photographers and TV cameramen recorded the event, which appeared on the evening news channels and in syndicated newspaper articles. Supermarket executives were more numerous than at the Hanratty's event, and the following day our brokers were besieged with orders. The food industry (or any other) had never seen introductory promotions quite like ours, nor had they seen the chunky, all-natural product we were promoting.

A month later, we repeated the spaghetti-sauce event in Los Angeles at a hamburger restaurant in Burbank. For this occasion the noted Hollywood composer Henry Mancini accompanied Joanne and Paul when they sang the spaghetti-sauce song.

THE DEMAND FOR Industrial Strength Sauce was so great that LiDestri had to run his production line around the clock, and he told an interviewer, "I guess you could say that Paul Newman's hunger that night in Westport revolutionized spaghetti eating in America."

The Salad Kings were now Pasta Kings, and our competitors were imitating us. We continually added new sauces to our shelf: Mushroom Marinara, Sockarooni, Bombolina, Fra Diavolo, Vodka, Roasted Garlic and Peppers, on and on. Paul and I were cracking ourselves up writing labels for these fast-moving sauces, like this one we wrote for our roasted garlic sauce:

ROASTED GARLIC AND PEPPERS

Once upon a time in the darkest of ages there lived a green grocer named Newmanezzer, who was famous for his virile garlic and voluptuous peppers. One starlit night, the Prince of the Garlic Bin climbed the fence and courted Princess Gwen Pepper in a heated mating dance that lasted a fortnight and wound up with a royal nuptial. A month later, as noted in the Baby Book of Records, Princess Gwen became the first stuffed pepper. It is her progeny who have danced their way into this bottle and onto your pasta.—*Newt Newmanezzer, XVI*

We are in the kitchen of a rented house in Ft. Lauderdale, where Paul is directing and acting in *Harry and Son*. It's the fourth time I have flown in from New York bearing popcorn samples. On previous visits, I have brought red kernels and black kernels, kernels from Iowa, Nebraska, Kansas, Texas, and Rhode Island, but none has satisfied Paul's finicky popcorn palate. Beer and popcorn have been lifelong staples of his diet, and whatever kernel is now going to fly the Newman's Own banner, it just better out-pop what Orville Redenbacher has on his shelf, a popcorn that Paul considers an insult to popcorn aficionados.

The usual tasting process on these *Harry and Son* occasions is to pop up a batch in the kitchen and invite the cast and crew for a communal tasting. Ellen Barkin, who is in the movie, matches Paul in her popcorn avidity.

What we are now tasting is a hybrid kernel grown by Wyandot, Inc., of Marion, Ohio, developed specifically to meet Paul's exacting requirements. The aroma is felicitous, and the kernels pop large and tender. Paul flicks melted butter and salt over the popcorn, and the sound of untidy lip smacking and teeth clacking fills the kitchen. "Man!" I exclaim. "Better than sex!" Ellen gives me a look. "Well," I amend lamely, "almost as good." No one disagrees. Paul and I dub it: Newman's Own Old Style Picture Show Popcorn, with this legend on the back of the bottle:

I'll tell you how bad it is. Nobody gets trusted with popcorn—except me. That includes the FBI, the IRS, Tiffany's, and concessionaires of any ilk. A good flick arrives on the local screen, you see ol' Newman scuttling across the lobby with a greasy brown paper bag of his homemade popcorn in one hand and—you guessed it—a machete in the other. Who's Who lists a lot of one-armed people in my hometown. They got caught trying to muscle their way into my greasy brown paper bag. The way I feel—they got off easy. They should be strung up.—*Col. P. L. "Pops" Newman*

To bring this cataclysmic event to the attention of the world, we schedule a popcorn pop-off on the grounds of the Westport Historical Society, everyone dressed in costumes circa 1880s. A madcap Dixieland band plays for the unveiling, and Paul once more courageously sings, this time my popcorn song, which again abuses Gilbert and Sullivan's "I Am the Very Model of a Modern Major-General."

Our popcorn makes you smile when you are suffering dyspepsia,
And it will goose your appetite when you have anorexia.
And all the horny Englishmen and Finns and overzealous Czechs,
Will find that Newman's Own is better than the kinkiest of sex!

It is the color of the sun and pops as white as falling snow,
And if your car should ever stall our hot popcorn will make it go,
The lights are low, your girl says no, and you are really through unless,
You feed her full of Newman's Own and turn her no into a yes!

Our blend of corn will most assuredly promote good fellow-ship,
And ev'rything is natural to clear up gout and nasal drip!

And now we tell you finally with candor and with clarity,
That you should buy a lot because our profits go to charity!

At our popcorn event, Paul and I, dressed in matching striped shirts and straw boaters, officiated over the wine bar; I filled each glass, which I handed to Paul, who in turn handed it to the guest. One lady, adoration in her eyes, asked Paul to stir the drink with his finger before handing it to her. "I would," he said, "but I've just been handling cyanide." Another lady asked him if he would remove his sunglasses so she could gaze at his celebrated blue eyes. "I'd be glad to, madam," he said, "but my sunglasses are attached to my belt and it would cause my pants to fall down."

WE ARE IN the Newman kitchen where Joanne has invited us to sample something she has concocted. Until now, Joanne has been both amused and impressed by us, more observer than participant, but now she places glasses in front of us and fills them from a pitcher containing a golden liquid. It is, quite simply, the best lemonade I have ever tasted. She has decided to let Newman's Own in on the secret recipe that has been zealously guarded by seven generations of her Georgia family. Right then and there Paul and I give it a name: Newman's Own Old-Fashioned Roadside Virgin Lemonade. Joanne questions the validity of "virgin," and I explain that the lemons will have never been squeezed before. Paul has the gall to proclaim, "It restores virginity."

———— ✦ ✦ ✦ ————

The marathon in Africa . . . I'm halfway out and barely chugging. Mountain coming! Liquid needed! What's around? Water's bitter! Beer's flat! Gator, Blah Blah! . . . Fading fast. Then a vision—sweet Joanna!— tempting me with pale gold nectar . . . lemon is it? By golly! Lemonade? No, Lemon Aid! . . . Power added: Asphalt churning . . . Cruising home

to victory! Hail Joanna! Filched the nectar (shameless hustler!)—in the
market—*Newman's Own!*

Paul enlists Whoopi Goldberg for the lemonade poster, and the
photo shoot is an event of unrelieved hilarity as Whoopi, dressed in a
virginal gown, is kneeling on a blue silk pillow at the base of a
waterfall, while Paul, in his Butch Cassidy getup, his red-stockinged
feet in a pool of water, pours the lemonade into a chalice Whoopi is
holding while she mutters swooningly, "I can feel it! I can feel it! It's
being restored! I'm becoming a virgin! Yes, yes, I'm a virgin again!" A
broad ribbon, supported by white doves, runs across her midsection,
carrying the boldly lettered words: **RESTORES VIRGINITY!**

In a newspaper interview, Paul was quoted as saying, "Joan
Collins was restored to virginity after drinking four quarts of it, and
Sylvester Stallone is on his forty-sixth case and still hoping." In
another interview, I was quoted as saying that the lemonade would
probably become "the official drink of Planned Parenthood."

The day after the horse ran away with him, Paul revisited the horseless popcorn wagon.

*E*ach of us in our own way was zealous and inventive about promoting our new popcorn offspring, but in one instance I was overzealous. I had located an antique popcorn wagon that in 1890 had originally been pulled by a horse. The ornate body of the wagon, enclosed with richly carved side panels and etched glass, accommodated the popcorn man, who was also the driver. The large popcorn maker was fueled from bottled gas. The popping corn was disgorged from the ornate silver top of the popper and filled a large space beside the popcorn man, who served his customers through a window.

Fortunately I knew Henry Stern, the New York City parks commissioner, who granted me a permit to station the wagon at a highly prized spot—one of the main entrances to Central Park at Sixtieth Street and Fifth Avenue. Paul was enthusiastic about this publicity coup, which he hoped would bring attention to our infant product.

My plan was that Paul would be the Popcorn Man and hand bags of popcorn through the wagon's window just long enough for the media to get its fill, then relinquish his role to a young man I had hired to stand by and take over, operating the wagon for the rest of the summer, charging a dollar a bag. For this event, though, Paul would distribute his largesse gratis.

I rented a horse named Daisy from a stable on Wooster Street that supplied many of the park's carriage horses. It was a nice-looking mottled gray horse that was brought to the park and attached to the wagon, just for looks since the wagon would not be leaving its location. When Paul's stint concluded, Daisy was scheduled to be returned to the stable.

Paul outfitted himself in an old-fashioned duster and a Newman's Own cap. The news media had been alerted. The old popping device worked perfectly, as a cascade of popcorn fell enticingly into a bin at the window. Paul entered the wagon from its rear door and began to fill paper bags emblazoned with NEWMAN'S OWN OLD STYLE PICTURE SHOW POPCORN.

The photographers started to set up as people entering the park presented themselves at the window to receive a bag from . . . PAUL NEWMAN! New York City is famous for the speed with which its citizens mobilize for an event—and they certainly mobilized for this one with the speed of a shooting star. God knows where they came from, but in no time there was a tangle of people trying to reach the movie-star popcorneer and his enticing handouts. They pushed aside, in fact abused, the media wretches and were less than gentle trying to get around Daisy, who tried to stand her ground but eventually did what disturbed horses do: she started to remove herself from the boisterous scene, and in doing so, of course, she was also removing Paul.

Paul shut down the window and tried to find the reins, which had been tightly attached to the driver's seat. I am not a horse person, but I knew that if I could reach Daisy, I might be able to grab her bridle and stop her. But there was no way to get to her. I yelled, "Whoa! Daisy, whoa!," but wiseacres in the crowd countered with "Giddyap! Daisy, giddyap!" Daisy pulled the wagon over the curb and around the corner in front of the Plaza Hotel and proceeded along Fifty-ninth Street.

I ran alongside the wagon, watching Paul who was, believe it or not, having the time of his life. He had unraveled the reins and was actually encouraging Daisy; I think he would have taken her all the way to Columbus Circle if she hadn't, by her own volition, pulled up at the rear of a line of carriages that were waiting to give rides in the park, just as she had numerable times in her line of duty.

I got to the rear door and pulled it open. Paul came out and a cabbie, who had slowed down, yelled, "Hey, Paul, needa taxi?"

We pushed into the cab and flopped onto the rear seat, both breathing hard.

"So, Hotchnik, have you got any more bright ideas?"

I gave him a look. He had lost his Newman's Own cap.

"You've got popcorn in your hair," I said.

*I*t's 1983, three days before Christmas, and the Lifeguard on Duty and the Assistant Lifeguard on Duty are under their beach umbrella, about to disseminate all the profits from their first full year of operation: $3,204,335 in sales that generated a profit of $397,000.

After the remarkable debut of our salad dressing, Paul and I cooked up a flow of products from the Newman's Own cornucopia: Light Italian Dressing, a full-bodied salsa with three degrees of heat, Bombolina Pasta Sauce ("The Intimate Companion Your Pasta Will Never Forget"), Caesar Dressing with Paul's marble bust on the label—an unending succession of dressings and sauces. For each new product, Paul changed his hat on the label. Now we are about to enjoy all the profits from those endeavors. We've got a pile of requests in front of us from worthy organizations. We are still amazed that our little business lark has made us rookie philanthropists, a triumph of irresponsibility over reason.

We start by making donations to major charities: Memorial Sloan-Kettering Cancer Center, Lahey Clinic, New York Foundling Hospital, Cystic Fibrosis Foundation, Society to Advance the Retarded and Handicapped, Harlem Restoration Project, American Foundation for AIDS Research, Alzheimer's Research, Flying Doctors, Literacy Volunteers, the Metropolitan Opera, Carnegie Hall, the Maritime Aquarium at Norwalk.

"You know, Hotch, sitting here giving away all our profits on

Hard at work thinking of a legend for Sockarooni spaghetti sauce.

December twenty-second totally changes my feeling about Christmas. Instead of it being steeped in mercantile greed, it is back to what I suppose was the real Christian objective, which was to hold out your hand to someone who is less fortunate than you are. Now people give with the expectation of getting something in return. Exchanging presents. What's Christmas got for me? But to give only for the sake of giving—Hotchnik, we're having a very good Christmas. You agree?"

"I guess so. You're talking to a guy who went to eleven different grammar schools, evading landlords. My idea of a Christmas present was a cheeseburger. But I sure like the way we're playing Santa Claus today."

With half our profits allocated to established charities, we now turn to the requests from obscure organizations that cannot generate the publicity that attracts donors. For example, we received this letter written by Sister Carol Putnam, a Sacred Heart nun who runs the Hope Rural School in Indiantown, Florida: "I am hunting desperately for help for a new bus. Ours does not pass inspection for the fall. A new bus costs $26,000. I have written to several sources and have gotten a 'no' so far. A bus will last us ten years and we cannot pick up the children without one."

Paul calls Sister Carol on the speakerphone. She tells us that Hope Rural, a school for the children of migrant farmworkers, might have to close down because its fourteen-year-old secondhand school bus has been condemned.

"Prior to Hope Rural School," Sister Carol tells us, "the children had no consistent schooling. They often labored in the fields alongside their parents. Many of them had never held a schoolbook or heard a nursery rhyme until the Hope Rural School, built by the migrant workers themselves, gathered up the children to attend classes during the picking season. But when our school bus was condemned this past summer by the state authorities, my worst fears were realized. With no bus to transport these children from their homes miles away, the school would be worthless, and many of the children would return to their hopeless lives in the fields."

After he hangs up Paul calls the Blue Bird Bus Company and informs them that he is sending a $26,000 check for immediate delivery. He is told there is a six-month wait, whereupon he asks to speak to the CEO who, fortunately, had recently seen *The Verdict*. The new bus arrived at the Hope Rural School two days later.

When a local reporter called Paul about the bus, Paul told him, "I never thought I'd get into science, but being able to turn salad dressing into a school bus—that's the kind of chemistry that tickles the fancy."

AFTER THE LAST dollar has been distributed, Paul leans back in his chair, a beatific smile on his face. "Who would have thought . . . and it's only the beginning. You're a philanthropist, Hotchnik. You realize? That St. Louis boy's come a long way."

Paul was referring to *King of the Hill*, a memoir I wrote about my boyhood in St. Louis when I was twelve years old, living by myself in a seedy hotel during the bottom of the Depression. Paul and Joanne had wanted to option motion-picture rights, provided I could flesh out my parents' roles for them. During the summer that I wrote about, my mother was in a tuberculosis sanitarium and my father was on the road trying to sell watches to people who were struggling to put food on the table. As for me, trapped in that miserable hotel room, I had no food and my rabid hunger actually impelled me to eat pictures of food that I cut out of magazines.

But for the screenplay, the more I tried to make my parents more of a presence, the more I knew I had to tell Paul that, reluctantly, I couldn't do it.

All he said was, "Pity."

YEARS LATER THE book was made into a film by Steven Soderbergh, with Robert Redford as executive producer. The movie was dominated by Jesse Bradford, a remarkable fourteen-year-old actor, and was rated one of the ten best films of that year.

EVERY DECEMBER, FOR twenty-four years, Paul and I shared a pastrami sandwich, a root beer, and licorice jelly beans while selecting a steadily increasing number of recipients of our profits, which reached a total of $260 million in 2007, the last year Paul participated.

*A*n intrepid reporter called Paul one day and asked about his cooking credentials, seeing as how he was up to his whiskers in the food business. Paul gave her a straightforward answer.

"My adult life has been spent in the family of women: my wife, Joanne; five daughters; my housekeeper, Caroline; and a succession of wire-haired terriers, all males who were immediately castrated upon arrival. No wonder I took to wearing an apron by way of disguise, lest I become a capon. This apron that started out as a protective measure became, over time, an excuse to pursue the discovery of culinary treasures.

"The discoveries result from my ability to establish a relationship with the food I'm about to cook. Have you ever had a meaningful conversation with a fillet of scrod? Or a dialogue with frog's legs?

"By way of preparation, I get ready by putting myself into a self-induced hypnotic trance, much in the same way the Shakirs trance themselves so that they can walk over hot coals and sleep comfortably on a bed of razor-sharp spikes.

"Once I'm in my trance, I hold the fillet of scrod in close proximity to my face, and pay attention. Sometimes I smell roses and think of flour. Sometimes I hear wedding bells, which translates to what? Mari-nade. Of course. Church music and bedsprings? Then I cook like Joanne, who laughs like a whore and sings like an angel.

"You may be a bit skeptical of my method—as have been many

before you—but to all those snicklers, snipers, and sniders I can only say that after the plates, knives, forks, napkins, and tablecloths are licked clean, nobody ever quarrels with the mystical, magical results of this intimate relationship between the chef and his victuals."

Despite that answer, the reporter continued, asking Paul the secret of his success.

Paul said, "I don't have the slightest idea. We have no plan. We have never had a plan. Hotch and I comprise two of the great witless people in business—none of this is supposed to work, you understand. We are a testament to the theory of Random—whatever that means!"

That testament to Random could be found on the sales graph that we had hung on the wall of our office, indicating sales from June to January. It had gone off the chart by the first of November and was headed up the wall. By January it was starting across the ceiling.

In addition to enjoying the phenomenon of our sales graph, we were also enjoying the phenomenon of customers writing us personal, rather intimate letters, which were certainly not the usual run of customer communication. The brokers said that, in their experience, letters written by customers were almost always complaints, but not ours. Our customers wrote to us as if they were members of an extended family. Praise and advice. Letters by the hundreds. In addition to letters of praise there were letters of gratitude and other such things.

Dear Sirs:

A miracle happened while eating a salad with your delicious dressing. Some dropped on my shoe. I ran and got a paper towel and rubbed it off—haven't seen a shine on my shoes like that for 81 years. Now I use it every day for shining my shoes, and putting it on my salad. Even tried it on furniture and it worked. So, you have a product to double your money. Your sales would go up ten percent if you let people know your dressing is good for shoes and furniture polish.

With your knowledge of products, I am sure you could make a cake out of it for shoe shining.

J.F.

Tucson, AZ

Dear Mr. Newman,

For a very long time I wanted to send you this letter, to let you know that your delicious "Paul Newman" Dressing is a household item in our home since it came to the market. As a matter of fact, this is the ONLY salad dressing we use. Even my husband, who fell into a coma 4 years ago and never recovered, raises his eyebrows when I feed him your dressing, that's how much he likes it. Well, you sure made this family happy, and I want to congratulate you for it.

Fondly,

G.G.

Plano, TX

Mr. Newman:

Last night my girlfriend treated me to a fabulous meal. It was quick and easy and quite good.

It consisted of spaghetti and green salad using your brand. All we did was pour your spaghetti sauce over pasta and make a tossed salad with your dressing. No fuss and very tasty. There's nothing to add so you can see why it was Q&E.

During dinner, my girlfriend mentioned you were a movie star. I would be interested to know what you've made. If you act as well as you cook, your movies would be worth watching.

Keep up the good work,

M.A.

Rancho Cordova, CA

P.S. Are any of your movies in VCR?

Paul was so delighted with this letter that he had it framed and hung it in the bathroom above the toilet.

From the get-go we had a policy of not advertising because a) Paul thought it was tacky, b) I discovered it was not always productive, and c) we couldn't afford the astronomically expensive campaigns to rival our giant competitors. Felicitously, we were receiving a lot of unsolicited accolades: *Consumer Reports* rates Newman's Own Microwave Popcorn number one over a field of thirty brands; *Los Angeles Magazine* awards Newman's Own Microwave Popcorn four stars and says it "deserves a popping Oscar"; *USA Today* rates Newman's Own Popcorn number one; *Entertainment Weekly* calls us the "tops of the pops"; *The Boston Globe* labels our Marinara Pasta Sauce the "hit of the week"; the *San Francisco Chronicle*'s Hot Stuff Awards rates Newman's Own All Natural Bandito Salsa above its eight competitors; *The New York Times* names Newman's Own "the preferred brand" in a tasting of sixteen marinara sauces; *The Sacramento Bee*'s six judges sample twelve national brands of chunky red salsa and rate Newman's Own at the top.

Each time Paul received one of these reports it was as if one of his children had brought home an A+ on an examination. Truth be told, Newman's Own had become a reality offspring, raised from the cradle and about to graduate magna cum laude. Paul no longer treated it as a lark. It was in stores everywhere in the United States and had voyaged onto grocery shelves all over Europe and Australia—in fact, we now had a factory in Scotland and another in Sydney in addition to factories in the United States.

To handle the burgeoning appetite for our pasta sauces, Cantisano had to build a new, significantly enlarged factory, thereby increasing the number of jars from one hundred twenty a minute to six hundred a minute, and they built a West Coast operation that supplies Newman's Own spaghetti sauces and salsa to the entire western part of the United States.

Ken's also built a new factory, increasing their production of salad dressing from sixty bottles a minute to four hundred, and going from an eight-to-five workday to around the clock.

IN ADDITION TO product awards, there were awards of distinction: Paul and I received Columbia University's Lawrence A. Wien Special Recognition Award for Outstanding Philanthropic Commitment; Paul was given the Jean Hersholt Humanitarian Award at the Academy Awards for his "commitment to philanthropy"; I collected on our behalf the James Beard Humanitarian of the Year Award at its annual gala in New York.

We also benefited from news reports like this one, which was sent to newspapers nationwide by PR Newswire:

> Today, it was learned that a truck containing a shipment of Newman's Own salad dressing was stolen last week, while en route from Southern California to Portland, Oregon. Other brands of salad dressing were on the truck as well but were untouched. The truck has been recovered, but the Newman's Own salad dressing is still missing at this time. The missing product includes 664 cases of Olive Oil & Vinegar, 238 cases of Balsamic Vinaigrette, and 344 cases of Family Recipe Italian flavors. Law enforcement authorities are baffled.
>
> When advised of the situation, Paul Newman said, "To be chosen and bought is one thing, but to be stolen before all the others is a

choice honor indeed. It's a great vote of confidence in our products—the other national brands of salad dressing must feel unwanted."

Not only were newspapers and magazines providing these unsolicited sales enchancers, but we were also benefiting from three events that were covered nationally. We had formed an entente with *Good Housekeeping* (4,534,700 readers) to sponsor an annual recipe contest which required entrants to use a Newman's Own product in their submissions. But instead of the customary cash awards, we offered the winners emoluments to give to their favorite charities. When the contest was first announced in *Good Housekeeping*, the "experts" (the same negative bunch who had doubted us from the beginning) scoffed at a contest that did not offer cash prizes. The naysayers warned us that we would get very few entrants. As it turned out, however, the Newman's Own Charity Awards tapped the *Good Housekeeping* readers' innate desire to help causes they cared about, and our contest attracted a huge response, second only to the Pillsbury contest which gave $1 million in cash to the winner. In our case, we

Hijinks at the Good Housekeeping *recipe contest.*

gave $50,000 to the charity of the winner and $10,000 to those of the four runners-up. The finalists were brought to New York from all over the United States, and at an elaborate luncheon, which we staged in Rockefeller Center's Rainbow Room complex, the winning recipes were served to Paul and Joanne, who, before an audience that included food critics, television reporters, and supermarket executives, rated each dish as prepared and presented by a Rainbow Room chef. All together—over the nine years that the contest flourished—there were twenty thousand recipe submissions and $2 million distributed to the winners, who bestowed their largesse on such charities as Habitat for Humanity, Special Olympics, Amnesty International, Child Abuse Prevention Effort, Multiple Sclerosis Society, the Starlight Foundation, and the Salvation Army.

A second yearly event that was consistently covered by the media was cosponsored by Newman's Own and John F. Kennedy Jr.'s *George* magazine. John and Paul both wanted to recognize corporate giving, and the George Award was created to honor the American company that best exemplified good citizenship through philanthropy, as demonstrated by monetary gifts or creative grassroots programs. A

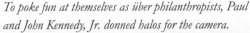

To poke fun at themselves as über philanthropists, Paul and John Kennedy, Jr. donned halos for the camera.

check for $250,000 was given to the charity of choice of the award recipient, who was chosen from hundreds of nominees.

The Newman's Own–George Awards were terminated upon Kennedy's tragic death.

A third annual event was the Newman's Own–PEN First Amendment Prize. For ten years, the $25,000 prize was awarded to a United States resident who had fought courageously, despite adversity, to safeguard the First Amendment right to freedom of expression as it applies to the written word. At the initial press conference announcing the award, Paul said, "One of the basic guarantees of the Bill of Rights is freedom of the press, freedom to write and publish without any abridgment. It is to safeguard and promote that freedom that we have established this award. To paraphrase Voltaire, it is our philosophy that although we may disapprove of what you write, we will defend to the death your right to write it."

Over the years, the award went to a Florida teacher, who succeeded in restoring literary classics, including the writings of Steinbeck, Chaucer, and Aristophanes, that had been banned from the classroom; an Arizona drama teacher, who resisted censorship of a play selected for a student production; a Denver bookstore owner, who successfully challenged a Colorado law barring stores that were open to children from selling novels such as *For Whom the Bell Tolls* because of its alleged sexual content; a journalist, who defeated a corporation's attempt to silence her written concerns about possible groundwater contamination caused by a local landfill; the president of a Texas college, who defended the production of Tony Kushner's play *Angels in America*.

$\mathcal{D}$ecember 1985, our fourth year of business, we have just finished shoveling four million bucks into scores of charities. We visited some of them, like the New York Foundling Hospital, a facility run by the Sisters of Charity, which cares for abandoned children, many of them suffering disabilities like Down syndrome and bipolar disorder. We had also visited the children's burn unit at the Cornell Medical Center, where children were recovering from catastrophic, life-threatening burns.

After we totaled up the exact amount that we had distributed, Paul said, "You know, Hotch, it's a great feeling, helping wonderful causes like this, but we should also be doing something of our own. I mean, these people we give to have all invented their mission . . . something they can identify with. We should have a cause we could build on—something very special to us."

"It's funny you bring this up, because leaving the Foundling Hospital, I got to thinking about how we could start up something like that."

"Absolutely right. We've struck gold, a couple of bumblers who stuck in their shovels and got lucky. Now let's run with it."

"You have something in mind?"

"No, not yet. Do we have any money left over?"

"Almost a million."

"We could start with that."

AT THE TIME, Paul was occupied with postproduction on *Harry and Son*, but a few weeks later he called. "I was shaving this morning when it dawned on me—a camp . . . a special camp for kids with life-threatening diseases like cancer. It afflicts more kids than any other disease. So let's build a wonderful camp tailor-made for these kids, one that will be free of charge—give these unlucky kids a little respite from the hospital and all that stuff."

As soon as he finished the final cut on *Harry and Son*, Paul sailed into his exploration of the camp project. He already had a name for it—the Hole in the Wall Gang Camp, named after the legendary gang of bandits in *Butch Cassidy and the Sundance Kid*—and he had a clear vision of the look of the camp: Butch and Sundance's village. Make-believe. An experience that would temporarily lift these children from the grimness of reality.

When asked in an interview about what had motivated him, Paul said, "I wanted, I think, to acknowledge Luck: the benevolence of it in my life, and the brutality of it in the lives of others, made especially savage for children because they may not be allowed the good fortune of a lifetime to correct it."

What Paul didn't acknowledge but what was, I suspect, an underlying factor was that both his mother and father had died of cancer.

Paul and I threw ourselves into this camp for afflicted children as wholeheartedly as we had charged into the salad-dressing challenge. We knew virtually nothing about either one of them, but our success as a couple of food mavens now emboldened us to meet this new challenge with confidence. But we had to start from absolute scratch.

If we were to succeed, we had to educate ourselves as to what kind of facility would be ideal for the incipient Hole in the Wall Gang Camp. We visited Camp Hemlocks, a Connecticut facility for the handicapped that didn't operate in the summer. It was an institutional structure, unadorned, a severe concoction of glass and steel. We could have operated our camp there during the summer months, but walking through those antiseptic buildings, Paul said, "Now we know we don't want our camp to look like that."

We flew out to California to visit Camp Good Times, which operated for several weeks for children with cancer. It was run by Pepper Abrams, who was very informative about the children and their illnesses, the camp programs, and the support staff that was needed. She also introduced us to the camp doctor, Dr. Stuart Siegel, who gave us insight into the medical aspect of their operation. But Good Times did not have its own campsite—it rented space from an existing camp.

We visited a camp in Blairstown, New Jersey, Memorial Sloan-Kettering's Happiness Is Camping. The doctor in charge was a pediatric oncologist, Dr. Paul Meyers, a very knowledgeable, engaging man who educated us on the special camping needs of children with cancer. Happiness Is Camping was a successful endeavor, but it was not built for the special needs of this population of children, and Dr. Meyers agreed that a specific camp such as the one we envisioned would be infinitely better.

Paul was impatient to get started and felt that the time had come for us to find a site where we could build the Hole in the Wall. To help us in this search we enlisted the assistance of Marc Nevas, the son of our lawyer, who ran a local real estate firm. The first site he found was north of New Haven, attractive land that had the drawback of being adjacent to a power line; we were advised that these power lines could possibly disseminate fields of energy that would be detrimental to the health of the campers. Marc showed us good acreage with a lake in Old Lyme, Connecticut, but its reputation as the original source of Lyme ticks discouraged us. We also looked at a facility in Torrington, Connecticut, owned by the YMCA, which had once been a Boy Scout camp, but it had deteriorated and was now up for sale. The buildings were rickety, and it had a lodge that was in precarious shape; what's more, the rotting dock was about to fall into the lake. But Paul, impetuous as usual, enthusiastically embraced an immediate plan to fix up the lodge, the cabins, and the dock. Work was started immediately on the lodge, a state-of-the-art kitchen was installed, the fireplace was reconstructed, and some serious money was expended.

"Paul," I said, "have you signed off on all this work?"

"Yup. We've got to get the camp up and running."

"But you're jumping the gun. We don't even have a contract to purchase the land site."

"You know how long those lawyers take, with their whereases and wherefores—I'll sign the contract when it's ready, but meanwhile we'll be getting everything started—"

"But we're talking about a large nut. The lodge with its kitchen will be at least $400,000, and then there's that long stretch of rotting dock, and all those cabins that are about to fall down—"

"Aw Hotch, it's the YMCA, for chrissake. Don't you trust anyone?"

"I trust you, my mother, and my children. Everyone else needs a contract."

"Well, pal, you need to loosen up. We're going to get this camp up and running. I'm leaving for Chicago tomorrow. Keep me posted."

And so he took off to make *The Color of Money* with Tom Cruise, without so much as a letter of agreement.

It was at this point that the YMCA people informed me that with the money that they would receive from us for the purchase of this property, they were planning to establish a camp for the Boy Scouts on the other side of the lake and share facilities with our camp. Although well-meaning, that was certainly not what we had in mind— children with cancer having to share a location with healthy, robust ones.

I called Paul on location in Chicago and told him about my meeting with the YMCA director.

"You're right," Paul said with a sigh, "it won't work. Get us out of it."

"Get us out of it? They've already rebuilt the lodge, installed a state-of-the-art kitchen, replaced the dock, and they're about to start on the cabins."

"The Boy Scouts can use it."

"But the Y doesn't have the money to run it."

"Well, maybe we'll send them some. Cheer up."

THE TORRINGTON FIASCO did nothing to dampen Paul's enthusiasm. He was often on the phone urging me to find suitable land for the camp, which had become an obsession. I did continue searching but with no success.

It occurred to me one day, however, that we were going about this ass-backward. I recalled Pepper Abrams's reliance on Dr. Siegel, whom she had called the "heart and soul of my camp." And then there was Dr. Paul Meyers, who was so vital to Happiness Is Camping. He had indicated to us that we should start with a doctor's medical input, then explore a campsite.

I called Paul. "Sounds right," Paul said, "but how do we find a doctor? That can be harder than a campsite."

"I heard about a Dr. Howard Pearson at the Yale-New Haven Hospital, who is the chairman of the Department of Pediatrics and a senior blood doctor in Connecticut. Thought I'd go talk to him."

"Good luck."

Dr. Pearson turned out to be a soft-spoken, attentive man with a wicked sense of humor and a tenderness about him that comes from many years of treating sick children. When I told him what we wanted to do, he leaned across the desk and said, "What do you need?" We didn't know that, providentially, Dr. Pearson was just completing a fourteen-year-term as chairman of the Department of Pediatrics at Yale, and that imminently he would have free time to devote to our undertaking.

In addition to becoming our camp doctor, Doc Pearson brought two other very important Yale people into our circle: Vince Conti, vice president of administration for Yale-New Haven, and Tom Beeby, dean of the School of Architecture. Conti's structured thinking and sense of organization was vital to the beginning of the camp, and Beeby brought an inspired concept to the design and building of the camp.

*O*nce Howard Pearson committed to being the camp doctor, all the other building blocks began to fall into place. Thanks to Ursula Gwynn, who had also helped organize our office, we found the campsite we had been seeking in the little town of Ashford, Connecticut, near the Massachusetts border, about equidistant from all the major population centers in the northeast, three hundred pristine, mostly level acres with a forty-five-acre pond, completely undeveloped, covered with exquisite wildflowers and frondescence.

Paul had just returned from making *The Color of Money*, and he walked the acreage with an ecstatic step, exclaiming over its possibilities, imagining how the campers-to-be would respond to it. I certainly shared his enthusiasm. Of course we realized that this site would require everything—electricity and phone lines, wells, septic tanks, roadways, fences, walkways, abridgments, landscaping, various permits, and every other amenity imaginable.

But none of this mattered to Paul. He was now on a mission that was unlike any of his others: his many forays into politics and other liberal causes; his devotion to auto racing; his attempt to resuscitate *The Nation* magazine; his resolve to write his autobiography, telling me several incidents he planned to write about, even producing five or six pages of what he said would start the first chapter. Paul had a distinctive lopsided style of writing that I thought would serve him well, but he said he was not remembering the past the way he wanted

Hotel —
fucking around
immortality, what?
PN

to, so he had arranged with his good friend Stewart Stern, the screenwriter on *Gamma Rays* and *Rachel, Rachel,* to interview the people whose names were on a list Paul had prepared: friends, relatives, actors and directors he had worked with, his Shaker Heights schoolteachers, Kenyon College professors, Actors Studio personnel, etcetera.

Stewart toured the country, conscientiously interviewing those on Paul's list; the tapes were transcribed and when the pages were assembled they made an impressive stack. I thought for sure that Paul would now find plenty to focus on, but when I asked him how it was going, he said it never got off the ground.

"Why?"

"Just generalities. No substance. I read through all that and it was just a mound of Jell-O."

We are all assembled in the conference room of Newman's Own, sitting at the Ping-Pong table (the net has been removed). In attendance are Dr. Pearson, Tom Beeby, Vince Conti, attorney Leo Nevas, and Simon Konover, head of a large construction company that bears his name. This is the team that hopefully will produce the camp.

Paul is popping up a batch of Newman's Own popcorn on his electric popper and sprinkling it with melted butter and salt. He fills bowls for everyone at the table.

"Fellows, this camp that Hotch and I are planning for kids who have cancer, we need to have it ready to receive these kids next summer, a year from now."

Their response was immediate and unanimous: that's impossible, out of the question.

"You mean," Beeby said, "from architectural plans to finished campsite?"

"Exactly."

"Paul, I never say never, but in this case I'm going to say it— never!"

"Tom, we are used to hearing that nasty word," Paul said, "from salad dressing to pasta sauce to popcorn and lemonade, that's all Hotch and I have heard. But we never gave ground. A year from now we're going to have a camp, and all of you are going to make it happen."

"Paul, it is now June 1987," Beeby said. "Do you honestly think we can have this whole camp built and running by June 1988? Let me read this list of things that will have to be done by then: septic tanks, freshwater wells, roads, telephone and electric lines, Olympic-size state-of-the-art heated swimming pool, twenty-two buildings—some of them, like the dining building, very complicated—thirteen log cabins made from special Canadian logs, the lake dredged, interiors finished, electronics, infirmary totally outfitted with all its complicated medical paraphernalia. We don't even have the architectural plans yet; normally it takes a year just to go from sketches to finished plans. All the permits that you will need from health inspectors, fire, sanitary, wetlands, and telephone grids, electrical plans, golf carts, trucks, office equipment, garden stuff, mowers, all that, computers. And then there's staffing—counselors, maintenance, kitchen, cooks, and also insurance. You'll be lucky to open in 1989."

Paul stuck to his guns. "We will be open in a year's time. When we started the salad dressing, Hotch and I had to slough off the discouragement and pessimism of the marketing and production experts who told us what we had to do and the big bucks it would cost, and now, once again we will make it happen."

Dr. Pearson said, "What if we do succeed in lining up a bunch of sick kids for next summer, and then have to disappoint them because you're not ready?"

"But if we are ready," Paul said, "then one thousand sick kids will have a summer that they wouldn't have otherwise. That's the risk—if we make it, they make it."

"There's no way that we can begin building until fall," Beeby said, "which means construction all through the winter. You know how tough winter can be up there. Blizzards and ice and the thermometer way down."

"We're a couple of gamblers on a roll," Paul said. "It's not the first time we've bet against the house."

"I'm all for the camp," Doc Pearson said, "and I agree—the sooner, the better. Cancer is the most prevalent childhood disease in the world. We could bring kids to the camp from all over this country, from everywhere. Seventy percent of the children don't make it, but thirty percent survive—in either case, if we get it right, we'll give them a wonderful respite from the hospitals. Some of these kids haven't had any experience outside their homes and hospitals."

"Paul and I will work with all of you on a daily basis," I said. "As you know we want the camp to resemble the western town in *Butch Cassidy and the Sundance Kid*. We want a very lighthearted, fun place with a kind of Alice in Wonderland feel to it. A fantasy place where the minute they set foot there, these poor kids will forget their past and current medical problems."

"A rough estimate," Conti said, "would be around ten million dollars."

"Well, by law Newman's Own can only donate half," Nevas said, "so five million will have to be raised from outside sources."

"We'll raise it," Paul said with conviction.

I looked at him quizzically, and he smiled.

"As Dean Beeby stated," Konover said, "I don't know if the giant earthmovers, steam shovels, backhoes, and all the rest can function in the severe cold, snow, and mud of the winter up there, but I will assign my best supervisor and push everyone to the limit."

"And I will get started on all the permits we need," Nevas said.

"Paul," Beeby said, "I may need you to meet personally with some of these small-town functionaries who like to throw their weight around. Small New England towns run things their own way."

"Just let me know what I can do and I'll do it," Paul said.

THERE WERE MEETINGS to obtain various permissions from local officials, but initially we didn't make much headway. The architects and the people from Yale met with four local officials in the back room of the library. The locals set up a lot of roadblocks and it appeared that they weren't going to be cooperative. A week later, however, when Paul went up to Ashford, the meeting had moved from the back room of the library to the school gymnasium, and there were four hundred people there instead of four. As for all the permissions we had requested, whatever Paul wanted was fine with them.

I HAD HAD two camp experiences in my life that contributed to my fervent involvement with the Hole in the Wall Gang Camp. When I was eight years old my mother was diagnosed with consumption (now called tuberculosis) and sent to the isolation section of the Fee Fee Sanitarium. In those days the children of tubercular patients were taken to the grounds of the sanitarium to spend a week in two huge tents, one for boys, the other for girls. The prevailing theory was that sun and fresh air would inoculate them against contracting the disease from their parents.

On the first day we were given blankets and told to sunbathe outside the tents under the brutal St. Louis sun. In charge of all the children was an administrator who timed us, thirty minutes on one side then thirty minutes on the other. We were given no sunscreen nor was there a doctor or nurse to monitor us during the process. I had red hair, freckles, and very pale skin and had never been away from the St. Louis streets.

At the end of the prescribed hour, we went back to our cots in the tent to rest, but ten minutes into my rest, I caught fire. Blisters the size of half-dollars covered my body and I spent the next several days in the infirmary.

My other camp experience I have chronicled in my memoir, *Looking for Miracles*. When I was sixteen, I bluffed my way into a lead counselor position at a camp where I was in charge of incorrigible, combative nine-year-olds who came from low-income problem families.

Those episodes fueled my urge now to help make this new camp happen—in a sense, to overcome the trauma of those former experiences.

ONE THING THAT was not going well was raising the five million needed for the camp's start-up.

"You announced you could raise it," I said to Paul.

"Our group needed a confidence builder."

"In other words, you lied."

"Did I raise their confidence or what?"

"You did. So now what?"

"I'll make some calls."

"I thought you made those calls."

"I did."

"So?"

"I'll make some more. I could swing it myself, but the frigging IRS won't allow it. Stop nagging. It'll happen."

"I can give you a five million dollar IOU."

"You brought it up."

"Five million makes me a little nervous."

"Cheer up. It could be ten."

A few weeks later, Paul's faithful mistress, Lady Luck, showed up and kissed him on the whiskers. She started things off with a phone call from a young man from Saudi Arabia, Khaled Alhegelan, who lived in Washington, D.C. He arranged to meet with Paul at our Connecticut office. He was afflicted with a rare blood disease, one that required all of his blood to be transfused regularly, and he wanted to know about this incipient camp he had heard about. He came up on the train, and Paul played Ping-Pong with him and discussed the model of the camp that was mounted beside the Ping-Pong table. What a boon, Khaled said, such a camp would have been to him as a seriously ill, isolated child—if one had existed. He said he would like to help with funding for the camp. Paul said, "Yup," which, translated, meant "I hear you but I don't expect much."

Twelve days later, Khaled phoned Paul and said that King Fahd had made a donation, but that to receive it we would have to attend a presentation ceremony at the Saudi embassy in D.C. Paul and I were stunned by the check made out to the Hole in the Wall Gang Camp that the ambassador, a Saudi prince, handed Paul—five million dollars! Since Saudi custom permits any citizen to petition the king for an audience, Khaled had requested this donation. Khaled's father had once been ambassador to Venezuela and Washington, which gave Khaled an edge, to say the least. The camp was now practically paid for; Khaled eventually became a valued member of the camp's board of directors.

THAT WINTER WAS one of the coldest on record—record snowfall, sustained subfreezing temperatures, ice storms, high-velocity winds, arctic conditions. There were few takers for the jobs at hand and finally we had to recruit Canadian workers who were used to frigid winter conditions. No matter how low the thermometer dropped or how dense the blizzard, these men constructed the cabins, which had a difficult tongue-and-groove assembly without nails. Paul and I plowed our way up to the camp one day through driving snow and ice and hosted a night for the Canucks at the Rusty Nail, a smoky tavern nearby that had pool tables, draft beer, and lumberjack food. Fast Eddie played pool with the guys and lost on purpose, tossed darts, filled them with Budweisers. He joined the workers as both cheerleader and coach, telling his merciless jokes, posing for instamatics, autographing shirts, menus, and even the top of a bald pate or two. Paul left them a dedicated, gung-ho team, ready to rush out for the Gipper through snowbanks and howling wind and score the winning touchdown in the final minutes.

At the same time, Doc Pearson was equipping and staffing a complete medical facility. The infirmary would contain emergency equipment to rival that of any hospital, and Doc would put into place protocols to cover almost every conceivable complication. There would also be a helicopter pad so that in a life-threatening emergency a child could be airlifted to the Yale-New Haven Hospital, which by air was only thirty minutes away. There would be doctors and a staff of nurses on duty around the clock, making it possible to perform procedures not available at ordinary camps. The infirmary would be able to give blood transfusions, platelet transfusions, and intravenous chemotherapy, which would enable really sick children to come to the camp.

AS SOON AS the winter relented, we were reinforced by an outpouring of spontaneous, unsolicited contributions: a local well digger donated four wells; 250 mattresses were contributed by a Hartford mattress company; members of the Connecticut State Legislature hosted a ball at which I was presented with a check sufficient to build the boathouse; Paul flew to St. Louis to see Augustus Busch (Budweiser sponsored Paul's race car) and walked away from the meeting with nearly $1 million, which covered the cost of building the centerpiece of the camp, the dining hall; the Eastern Airlines Silverliners (retired flight attendants) raised $11,000; the U.S. Army Corps of Engineers dredged the entire lake and repaired the dam; the U.S. Navy Seabees built a network of bridges across wetlands and marsh areas that entirely circumnavigated the camp. Members of the Connecticut Swimming Pool Association, usually fierce competitors, banded together to donate the swimming pool: one company dug the hole, another sprayed the gunite, another did the tiling, another installed the heating equipment, another built the bathhouses—an amazing feat of cooperation that resulted in a state-of-the-art Olympic-size swimming pool that would have cost approximately $1 million. On its completion, all the members of the association held a baptism party at the pool, which was blessed by a consortium of clerics, a priest, a rabbi, and a minister. It was a joyous occasion, this magnificent pool created by competitors who, on that day, glorified charity. The next day, they all went for one another's throats in happy competition, as usual.

All through that spring we were flooded with contributions from firefighters, hairdressing salons, community associations, and school groups, who staged walkathons, talkathons, jumpathons, bikeathons, every conceivable "thon" except studyathons. An eight-year-old boy sent in $5.40, which he had earned from operating a lemonade stand the previous summer.

*O*ne April day in 1988, Paul and I packed a picnic lunch and drove up to the camp. We hadn't been there since the last of the fierce March snowstorms and were anxious to see if the camp could possibly be ready to receive the first children, who were due to arrive the middle of June.

Paul pulled up in back of the dining hall, which on our previous visit had been half finished but now towered majestically over the other camp structures. We entered by a rear door and walked slowly toward the center of the beautiful circular expanse with its cathedral apex. The floor, composed of a unique mosaic of wood ends, was only half finished but it did not lessen the impact of this building, which would be the centerpiece of the camp.

We stood in the center of the floor, turning slowly in startled admiration of what we were seeing. Through the tall windows we could see the finished gymnasium with its bark-covered columns, and to our left a file of arts and crafts structures, all designed in a homogeneous western style. And beyond that, the OK Corral, a trading post that masqueraded the camp's mini-hospital. Farther along, we could see the circles of log cabins, beautifully constructed by the Canadians. Where only a year ago there had been barren land, now there was this glorious make-believe town, this fulfillment of Paul's unrelenting vision.

Paul thrust his hand at me and I grasped it, bonding us in a heartfelt handshake that was a celebration of what we had accomplished. Then Paul began to laugh, a deep, roaring laugh, and I joined his laughter, uncontrollable laughter, doubling us over, capturing our breath, tearing our eyes, laughing in joy, the joy of this splendid moment, when our crazy adventure with that bottle of salad dressing had miraculously produced this fantasy for sick children.

The majestic dining hall.

$\mathcal{F}$rom the day the ten million was securely in the bank, we went full speed ahead: hiring a camp director (through a search committee); recruiting counselors from universities; staffing the kitchen; arranging for horses; equipping the boathouse with rowboats, canoes, and fishing tackle; outfitting the arts and crafts buildings, the office, the gymnasium, the children's cabins, and the library; and installing furry and feathered residents in the petting zoo.

The last workmen, the bulldozers, and the construction trailers pulled out virtually as the first children began to arrive in June 1988. And there we were that first day, standing in the reception area, waiting for our first hundred kids to arrive. Doc Pearson, the nurses, and all the new counselors were there, prepared for an exuberant welcome. Paul was as nervous as a groom. But it didn't take long for his nervousness to devolve into disappointment. Arriving buses were half empty; some parents did not show up with their kids. Instead of a hundred, there were only forty-six. Paul was downhearted. He went over to Doc Pearson.

"We're a bust, Howard. If they don't come when there's no charge, when the camp is this terrific, and we have you and nurses and that little hospital equipped with everything, then I guess we're not going to make it."

"Now, Paul," Doc said, "what you have here is something new and it'll take awhile. Most of these kids have never been away from their parents, except for hospitals. But when word gets around from parents whose kids just showed up, then other parents will trust us. Besides, I think your new counselors would have been overwhelmed with a summer of one thousand kids. Now, with half as many, they'll gradually learn how to cope and be better able to handle a full load. Stop worrying. We're going to have a full house in no time."

Doc was right. Like our salad dressing, it took awhile for the camp to catch on—288 the first year, 1,000 the next year, then a waiting list, year after year after year.

WE ANTICIPATED THAT the atmosphere of this camp for kids with cancer would have a subdued hospital aura—kids in treatment for leukemia, undergoing radiation, chemotherapy, and other forms of medication, many bald, some without limbs, some with catheters in their chests. The wonderful revelation was that this was not at all a somber hospital-type atmosphere but a joyful one for the children and for us. These children had the time of their lives from the moment they arrived, even those in wheelchairs or on crutches—the ones who could walk pushed the ones who couldn't, the ones who had hair painted the heads of the ones who had lost their hair. It was a happy release for all of them. They'd been pent-up in hospitals, living in communities where they were outcasts, where other kids made fun of them. They couldn't play sports. They were denied so many things. Now suddenly the camp put them in an environment with kids who were in the same boat they were in. And they are being told, Yes, get up on this horse, you *can* ride a horse. We may have to hold you, walk with you, but you *will* ride a horse. Come out on the boat. You *can* catch a fish. This was all new to them. They were having fun.

THE HOLE IN THE WALL turned out to be the gestating seed of a crop of siblings that have sprung up all over the world, providing

Paul with so many offspring, like the old lady in the shoe, he didn't quite know what to do. First came a query from an entrepreneur named Charles Wood, who wanted to establish a camp like ours near Lake Luzerne, New York. His intention was to convert a deserted dude ranch into a camp for kids up to age seventeen. Our camp only went to fifteen. Paul and I were delighted to assist him. We advanced him a million dollars in seed money, which became our modus operandi with all the new camps that followed. He named his camp the Double H Hole in the Woods Ranch.

All the new camps came up with their own names, but we formed an Association of Hole in the Wall Gang Camps to which all of them belonged and which set standards that had to be maintained. There followed the Boggy Creek Camp, headed by General Norman Schwarzkopf, built near Orlando, Florida; the Barretstown Camp, County Kildare, southern Ireland; L'Envol, near the Fontainebleau forest, just south of Paris; the Painted Turtle Camp, near Palmdale, California; Victory Junction Gang Camp, Randleman, North Carolina; Jordan River Village in lower Galilee on the Jordan River; the Over the Wall Gang Camp in the United Kingdom; Bátor Tábor Camp in Hungary; Dynamo Camp in Italy; Flying Horse Farms Camp in Ohio; Roundup River Ranch in Colorado. In 2008, the conglomerate of camps served over 44,000 sick children.

There are additional camps in development in Sedona, Arizona; Ann Arbor, Michigan; Philadelphia, Pennsylvania; Seattle, Washington; and Hokkaido, Japan. Also, for the past eight years the association has served more than 2,700 children in Botswana, Lesotho, Malawi, Namibia, South Africa, Thailand, Uganda, Vietnam, Ethiopia, and Cambodia.

Paul and I often flew to these camps in their embryonic stages to offer our assistance. On one such occasion, the Ritz Hotel in Paris was staging a formal fund-raising event for the beleaguered L'Envol, our camp in the south of France. My wife, Virginia, and I met up with Paul and Joanne at the Ritz on the day before the black-tie event. We were joined at dinner that night by my old friend Jack Hemingway,

Ernest's eldest son, and his wife, Angela. During dinner, Paul told us about his first stay at the Ritz with Joanne.

"We had just visited London," Paul said, "where we stayed at the Savoy, but we were under such siege by the vicious London paparazzi and swarms of avid fans that we couldn't leave the hotel. We were going to Paris next, so playing it smart, I made arrangements for us to enter the Ritz by an obscure employee entrance on the Rue Cambon. This entrance took us through the basement and all the kitchens, finally landing us in the lobby. One of the hotel's functionaries was there to greet us. 'I guess we gave 'em the slip,' I said to him, exuding cleverness. 'Who would that be, sir?' 'Why your terrible paparazzi and all the fans with their autograph books.' 'Well, sir,' he said, pointing to the entrance, 'as you can see no one is there.' "

The following day Paul took me aside and read the little speech he had written for the evening.

"How about I do it in French?"

"You speak French?"

"Well, my accent's pretty good and I could have it spelled out phonetically."

"Great idea. The French are very snobby about their language and they like when you speak it."

I asked Frank Klein, the president of the Ritz, to recommend someone to assist Paul, which he did. She translated the speech to French and spelled out each word phonetically. Paul practiced reading it all through the afternoon, and his pronunciation was indeed pretty good. I was sure the crowd would be pleased.

The benefit assemblage was as soigné and glittering as any Ritz gathering could possibly be. If only the cost of the jewels and designer gowns and furs could have been donated to L'Envol, all its financial troubles would have disappeared.

Just before the program began, Paul went to the men's room where he took off his jacket and stuffed a hand towel under each arm to keep his nervous perspiration from penetrating his jacket. By nature, Paul was very shy and totally uncomfortable at having to appear before an audience like this, and it always made him sweat. But when he performed onstage, his shyness retreated into the character he was playing. At this moment, however, with Paris's high society awaiting him, Paul had no cover.

He was introduced to a warm reception and then, looking at the paper with the phonetics on it, he said, "*Mesdames et Messieurs*" and the guests murmured their approval. Paul studied his paper for a moment, looked up at the expanse of expectant faces, then stuffed the paper in his pocket and switched to a brief few sentences in English before thanking everyone and going to his seat. He didn't even venture "*merci.*"

*I*n the original architectural schematic for the Hole in the Wall Gang camps, a theater had been included, but the board of directors had become wary about our profligate ways and had decided to save the money earmarked for the theater and incorporate its function into the dining hall. As a couple of theater people, Paul and I were unhappy with the acoustics and performing area for the camp's theatrics. The children were trying to rehearse their skits and little musicals while the dining-hall crew was mopping the floor and setting up the tables.

So, as usual, we resorted to shameless expedience and deviousness to achieve beneficial results. On one of our visits to the camp, Paul noticed that a large piece of machinery was excavating at one end of the lakefront. It so happened that the dimensions of the theater had originally been staked, in anticipation of the day when a theater might be approved. Paul and I commandeered the operator of the digger and had him transfer his digging to the theater site, where he scalloped out the foundation.

At the next board meeting, I reported that this mistaken excavation had created a hole that could cause trouble—what the law calls an "attractive nuisance"—and that's how the camp acquired a state-of-the-art, 280-seat theater that quickly became the focal point of the camp's activities.

. . .

The annual cast photo featured Paul and Joanne, James Naughton, Tony Randall, and, lower left, Chita Rivera, with a couple of costumed campers in the foreground.

EVERY CAMP SESSION, there was a "stage night," when the children entertained one another with musical performances and quirky skits dear to the hearts of campers. At one such stage night I turned to Paul and said, "Why don't we have a benefit at the end of the summer like these stage nights, only with Broadway and Hollywood stars interacting with the kids?"

"And who would come to this?"

"People who like theater and want to support the camp. We could give them a hearty lunch in a big tent with a fun auction and a good show at a thousand bucks a pop."

"And what stars would come to perform in our little camp theater way up in Connecticut, three hours from New York, with no press or TV?"

"Stars like you and Joanne and the ones you'd invite. I would write and produce it. What do you say?"

"I say you're nuts. You'll get no stars and no audience. I'll help you even though I think Lady Luck's gonna kick your ass on this one."

I decided to invite a dozen stars in the hopes that two or three might say yes. Besides Joanne and Paul, the list included Judy Collins, Phylicia Rashad, Kathie Lee Gifford, James Naughton, Barbara Rush, B. D. Wong, Savion Glover, Jason Robards, Cy Coleman, dancers from *Cats*, and that incomparable New York balladeer Bobby Short. To my amazement and consternation, they all accepted. What's more, every seat in the house was sold. The show ran more than two hours and the auction was a big success—Kathie Lee Gifford even auctioned off the necklace she was wearing.

In the eighteen years of those September galas, we had remarkable performances from Danny Aiello, *Sesame Street*'s Big Bird, Kevin Kline, Gene Shalit, George Shearing, Alec Baldwin, Rosemary Clooney, Tony Randall, Amy Grant, Meryl Streep, Bruce Willis, Bernadette Peters, Kim Basinger, Michael Bolton, Ann Reinking, Melanie Griffith, Joan Rivers, Glenn Close, Marisa Tomei, Bill Irwin, Whoopi Goldberg, Harry Belafonte, Nathan Lane, Julia Roberts, Carole King, the cast of *Stomp*, Christopher Reeve, Chita Rivera, Isaac

Stern, Phoebe Snow, Jack Klugman, Lillias White, Willie Nelson, Rosie O'Donnell, Robin Williams, Eartha Kitt, Jerry Seinfeld, Joshua Bell, Kristin Chenoweth, Michael J. Fox, Gregory Hines, Jerry Stiller, Ben Vereen, Mikhail Baryshnikov, plus jazz bands, dance groups, gospel singers, acrobats (AntiGravity), magicians—and Paul played a leading role in all of them.

Performing in sketches and musical numbers with these stars gave the children moments to cherish forever. And the performers say that the children have given them moments that they too would never forget.

All together, the eighteen galas I wrote and produced raised $11,187,490 for the camp and played to 5,900 people.

*P*aul and I were sitting outside the camp theater, going over his part in that evening's gala performance—my bowdlerization of *The Wizard of Oz*, with Savion Glover as the Tin Man, Tony Randall as the Scarecrow, a camper as Dorothy, and Paul as the Cowardly Lion.

Paul was growling through his song, growling better than Bert Lahr in the original.

"I'm going to cry after the song," Paul said.

"The more tears the merrier," I said.

We sat for a spell, enjoying the warm September sun. From within the theater, strains of "Hey, Look Me Over" floated out to us.

"I'm going to burn my tuxedo," Paul said.

"You're going to what?"

"Burn my tux."

"Why?"

"Two black-ties last week. I used to like my tux—no more."

"What happened?"

"All those tux benefits. They buy a table, display all their jewels and diamonds, and get up and go to the powder room as often as possible so everyone can see their Chanels and Yves Saint Laurents and the loops of Cartier around their necks. And when I have to go to the mike and say some banal something or other, everyone's yapping and paying no attention. I used to like my tuxedo. It's over. It's gonna be toast."

"You really mean it, don't you?"

"Up in flames."

"All right. Tell you what. Next week, I'm going to have a cookout in Westport for tonight's production crew—bring your tux and we'll have a proper cremation."

The evening of the cookout, Paul brought his tux on a hanger and hooked it on the back of his chair. I had split Cornish hens, corn, and Italian sausages on the grill. I clanged a glass for attention.

"We are all gathered here tonight to commemorate the passing of Paul's tuxedo. He would like to say a few words for the departed."

Paul picked up his tux and held it beside him. He praised the tux for its faithful service at funerals, Academy Awards, benefits, weddings, banquets, inaugurations, bar mitzvahs, anniversaries, premieres, and such, but he said the day of his tux had come and gone and now it must be dispatched to the great Tuxedo Junction in the sky.

He carried the tux to the driveway where I had arranged a small funeral pyre. He lovingly placed it on top of the pyre and put a match to it. He raised his glass and drank to his departing tux, and so did the rest of us. I thought it was quite wonderful, drinking in the firelight to Paul's deceased tux.

From that day on Paul was able to turn down all black-tie events by explaining that his tuxedo had passed on.

 lthough Paul did accept a few awards over the years, he rejected most attempts to honor him for his acting and his philanthropy. When the prime minister of Canada invited him to a glittering annual event to be the recipient of Canada's highest honor, Paul politely turned him down. A week later, the prime minister asked Paul to reconsider in light of the fact that past recipients were such luminaries as the pope, Mother Teresa, and Prince Charles.

"I appreciate the honor," Paul said, "but, look, I'm giving this money away out of a kind of personal conviction and I don't think I should take some kind of public award for it. I just think it's something I should be doing, and the minute I stand up and say, 'Look at me, I'm giving away all this money . . .' "

"But what about Mother Teresa? What about the pope?" the prime minister asked.

"Maybe the pope needs the publicity more than I do," was Paul's rejoinder.

There was one award, however, that he enthusiastically accepted. It was the Kennedy Center Honor, which was conferred on Paul and Joanne in 1992. This annual event plaudits six distinguished artists, who do not perform at the event but are honored at a dinner hosted by the secretary of state, followed on the succeeding evening by a program on the main stage of the Kennedy Center hosted by the president. Prior to Paul's event, my friend, the composer Cy Coleman and I were contacted by the producer of the program, George Stevens Jr., who wanted our suggestions as to what he could present on the stage that would have emotional relevance for the Newmans.

I said that in my view nothing would be more appropriate or moving than surprising Paul and Joanne with a contingent of children from the Hole in the Wall Gang Camp singing, "If There Were More People Like You," which Cy had composed with the lyricist Dorothy Fields. This song had been sung by the children at the conclusion of all the camp galas, and I knew it would mean a lot to Paul, the camp being his proudest achievement, more so than anything related to his movies. Stevens wanted the kids to appear as a surprise, which required a great deal of surreptitious maneuvering. Twenty children, their parents, and supervising camp counselors were to be transported, housed overnight, brought to the Kennedy Center for staging and rehearsals with the orchestra, all of it kept under the Newmans' radar.

The morning of the Kennedy Honors, however, the surprise almost got blown. Cy and I met for breakfast in the dining room of the Ritz-Carlton, the headquarters for the event. Paul, of course, did not expect us to be in Washington for the occasion, so when he came into the dining area for breakfast, prior to his morning jog, he wanted to know why I was there. "We're on the Kennedy Honors Artists

Committee," Cy said, quickly providing us with a cover. "We nominate the honorees." Paul had breakfast with us and went off to jog, none the wiser.

It worked beautifully. Paul and Joanne along with the other honorees—Lionel Hampton, Ginger Rogers, Paul Taylor, and Mstislav Rostropovich—occupied boxes alongside President and Mrs. Bush. A twelve-year-old camper, Wil Demers, a virtuoso horn player who had performed with Paul at the camp galas, was spokesman for the children, who sang directly to Paul and Joanne:

If there were more people like you
Oh, what a fine world this would be
For you take time to see things
Most people don't take time to see.

If there were more people who do
There would be much less to be done,
We could right now so many wrongs
If we fight for rights to be won

If there were more people who care,
There would be fewer people to care for,
More people of worth,
Good people worth our saying a prayer for,
Less people who don't
There would be more people who do,
If there were more people like you!

Paul was totally surprised and overjoyed at this public but intimate moment. Tears ran unabashedly down his cheeks. He extended his arms toward the children symbolically, embracing them from his lofty perch. It was a glorious moment for Paul, for the children, and for the three thousand inspired members of the audience.

*I*t was gradual but noticeable when Paul started to withdraw, to ease away from commitments, from certain incursions on his time, from physical demands.

To begin with, he arranged to meet me in our Newman's Own office one day and said, "Hotchnik, it's time we got out of the grocery business, you and I, and brought in professionals."

We were standing in front of our desk and I was startled by his abruptness. We had been running Newman's Own for fourteen years. I said, "When would that be?"

"Now."

"Today?"

"Yep. We're too big a business for a couple of dilettantes."

"Who's going to take over?"

"I've hired the business consultant who ran the IBM seminar with us and our brokers."

"Has he ever run a business like this?"

"No, but he knows all the basics."

That's all there was to it. No preamble. No good reminiscence. Nothing. Paul may have been influenced by the fact that recently his friends Ben and Jerry had retired from running their ice-cream company and turned it over to a hired hand. I thought about the business consultant Paul had hired, a didactic, humorless company man who sang operatic arias while reading spreadsheets. But Paul was right, it was time for us to bow out. And like removing a Band-Aid, do it very quickly so it won't hurt so much.

"We will still write the legends for new products," Paul said, "and sort of keep an eye on things."

"We're giving up our office?"

"No—we're setting up a new office for him, and I'm setting up one for me across the hall. You'll be on your own here."

The business consultant, as it turned out, needed a business consultant. Paul quickly replaced him with Tom Indoe, who had extensive experience in the food business and also had the personality and attitude that was a fit for our unconventional company.

THAT WAS THE first sign of Paul's withdrawal. He continued to do a few movies, but *Twilight* and *Message in a Bottle* and *Where the Money Is* all seemed like films that he took on to keep busy, rather than ones he was really into.

He spent more and more time at the Connecticut camp. He was heartened by the fact that the rate of survival for the children, which was 30 percent when the camp began, had now, thanks to medical advancement increased to 70 percent. Paul built a cabin on the edge of the lake, across from the camp, where he and Joanne would occasionally go to live simply and fend for themselves. He'd ride his bike to the dining hall at noon and have lunch with the kids; in the evening he often sat on the cabin's porch and cast a line into the lake.

One day I was walking to the dining hall with him when a little camper took his hand and said, "You know, Mr. Newman, all year long, this is the week I live for."

Paul looked at me. "That's it!" he said. "That's the applause. That's what you really want in life."

FOR A WHILE, Joanne took over the artistic direction of the Westport Country Playhouse, and Paul invested time and considerable money in rebuilding it and an adjacent decrepit restaurant. He momentarily vitalized the playhouse by performing as the Stage Manager in a revival of *Our Town*, a role which he repeated on Broadway.

When he was approaching eighty, Paul had announced that he was giving up acting. I asked him about that and he said it was mainly because of his increasing inability to remember his lines. "I'm not going to wind up like Marlon with my lines posted on cards all over the set," he said.

I asked him how it happened that he could remember the long monologues of *Our Town* but not the abbreviated takes of a movie. "Because in *Our Town* they are set pieces, not the give and take of conversation. I deal with the *Our Town* monologues at my own pace, but movie dialogue forces me to instantly respond to another actor, and that's the rub."

Despite his avowal, Paul had a momentary resurgence of spirit, solidly performing a supporting role in *Road to Perdition*, and, later on, another acting surge as a wonderfully bizarre bearded old man in *Empire Falls*, for which he won an Emmy. Aside from providing the growling voice of a Hudson in *Cars*, he never again performed— except for the camp galas where he still romped through the outrageous parts I created for him to perform with the children.

He continued to follow his racing team to the tracks around the country, and in the summer of 2007, at eighty-two years of age, he raced at Lime Rock.

Every year, as usual, we divvied up a pastrami sandwich and distributed millions to charities that we chose from qualified lists, but Paul was increasingly concerned about fulfilling all the new, inhibiting requirements of the IRS—inhibiting in the sense that our donations had to be less spontaneous and more rigidly contributed to be sure that we were operating within the IRS parameters.

It was at this point that Newman's Own was reorganized. A board of directors was installed with a very knowledgeable chairman,

Robert Forrester, who organized the charitable arm of the company into a foundation.

We continued to react to global disasters through the foundation with large, immediate donations: victims of the tsunami, the famine in Ethiopia, Hurricane Katrina, the 9/11 fund for firemen's widows.

Paul backed off from doing the product legends, relegating his participation to editing the ones I now had to write solo. But he did collaborate with me on two celebrity-based cookbooks published by

Simon and Schuster, one for children, the other for purchasers of Newman's Own products.

The last legend I wrote that I submitted to Paul was for Newman's Own new line of breakfast cereals. We were sitting in his new office. I had turned mine into an Egyptian sarcophagus, complete with hieroglyphics depicting Paul and me attended by handmaidens and me as a camel with Paul in the saddle. Paul read the legend I handed him very deliberatively, smiling along the way.

———— ✦ ✦ ✦ ————

There was a young boy named Timmy who had a very round tummy. Timmy hated his tummy and was so mortified he fled to the closet to consult with his favorite Teddy Bear who said, "Timmy, you've got to reduce your girth and regain your mirth. Let's consult Doctor Bear who's over there."

Doctor Bear poked his finger into Timmy's tummy and said, "Gushy. What do you eat for breakfast? Cereals, said Timmy. Two bowls of cereals. "Aha!" exclaimed Doctor Bear, "frosted this and sugary that. No wonder!"

But they're yummy, said Timmy. "But look at your tummy! Cereal can be yummy but sugar is rummy, so tell your mummy that Newman's Own now has cereal that's all natural, just sweet enough with natural stuff."

So Timmy told his mummy, the new cereals were yummy, Timmy lost his tummy, and any kid who's still eating those sugary, sugary cereals is, as Doctor Teddy says, "A first-class dummy!"

———————————————

"Okay," Paul said, "but can't we get a better kid word than 'mortified'? That's too grown up. Let's think of something . . ."

We strained for a good substitute, but none made the cut.

"Okay, then," Paul said, "let's make up a word, a good kid word." We thought. And thought.

"I've got one," Paul finally said. "Mortiflated."

And that's the word that's on all our cereal boxes today, although mothers have trouble explaining it to their kids.

PAUL HAD ONE unwavering source of pleasure—his two little grandsons, Peter and Henry, the progeny of his daughter Lissy and her husband, Rafe. They live in the original house on the opposite side of the drawbridge that Paul had suspended across the Aspetuck River. Paul doted on his grandsons and even carried their pictures in his pocket, displaying them at every opportunity like grandpas everywhere.

ONE DAY IN early September 2007, Paul called suggesting lunch at the Dressing Room. We sat at the bar and ordered our usual hamburger nestled under sautéed onions, divided in two. "I've been thinking about the gala," he said. The annual gala was ten days away. "What number is this?"

"Our eighteenth year."

"Well, I think maybe the audience is tired of all those spoofs you do of Broadway musicals and tired of me doing them, mostly in drag." He took a big bite of his burger and anointed it with a gulp of iced tea. "My liver can't handle beers at noon anymore," he said. Over the years I had written skewed versions of musicals like *Annie* (Paul was Annie), *My Fair Lady* (which became *My Fair Laddie* with Bruce Willis as a street urchin, Meryl Streep as Henrietta Higgins, and Paul as Alfred Doolittle, an auto racer), *The Sound of Music* (Paul was Liesel),

The Music Man (Paul was the mayor's wife), *Alice in Wonderland* (Paul was the Mad Hatter), *Snow White and the Seven Dwarfs* (Paul was Sleepy) *Guys and Dolls* (Sarah Brown), *Peter Pan* (Tinkerbell).

"You mean beginning next year?" I said.

"No, this year. It's time we do something else."

"But the gala's only ten days away and I've already knocked out a spoof of *Annie Get Your Gun*. Renee Zellweger is set for it. And you'll be Big Chief Sitting Cow."

He scraped up a forkful of the remaining onions on his plate and slathered it on the last bite of his burger. "Well, we've got time—how about something else?" He turned and faced me. He was gaunt and pale, and his habitual horn-rimmed glasses were a little askew on the end of his nose. "You'll think of something. You always do."

He got up from his barstool but with difficulty. I gave him a hand. His back was killing him. We went out to the parking lot. He walked stiffly, holding a hand pressed against his back. "This damned sciatica," he said, "I haven't been sleeping much because of the pain."

"How about a massage?" I said. "I know a good masseur—"

"Thanks, Clea knows someone, but I don't think it would help with this."

I got in my car and watched as he stiffly and painfully got into his car and drove off.

I sat behind the wheel for quite a while. From the diminished look of him, his reduced voice, the pain and stiffness he attributed to sciatica, the abruptness of his pronouncement about the gala, there was no doubt in my mind that this was Paul's way of telling me that this was his last gala.

I started my car, having decided that this would also be my last gala. I think he was telling me, in effect: We created this, now let's pull out together. I knew I could never do a gala without Paul.

At that year's finale, as I had for eighteen years, I announced the day's take to the audience—more than a million dollars—and lauded the performers and the children for their contributions. And I announced that this was my final gala. As the cast began to sing the closing song, "If There Were More People Like You," I started to make my way off the stage. Paul came over, stopped me before I reached the wings, and gave me a profound hug.

I stood in the wings. This was a painful moment for me. I had invented this gala: the children opening the show with new lyrics I wrote to old show tunes; movie stars and Broadway stars doing sketches with the children; Chita Rivera, Gregory Hines, Anne Reinking dancing; Isaac Stern and Joshua Bell and Rosemary Clooney captivating the audiences; children telling their sad, brave stories; Jerry Seinfeld and Robin Williams eliciting laughter; the backstage team I had assembled that happily showed up year after year; two eight-year-olds, bald from chemo, playing a flute duet; the teenager, blind from a tumor, performing her own composition on the piano; the sadness of losing twelve-year-old Wil Demers, a wonderful horn player who had a talent big enough for a bright future.

As I walked away from the theater into the summer night, I mourned the loss of never again enjoying a September when Paul and I collaborated on that year's nonsense. The joy of our rehearsals, of making the impossible possible.

Sad.

*D*uring that fall, Paul kept busy and made plans for the coming year. He planned to direct *Of Mice and Men* at the playhouse, and he had scheduled two races at Lime Rock, driving a special Corvette that his team had prepared for him. He relished telling me about the mechanical minutiae that made this Corvette so special. His enthusiasm was heartening, but the reality of how he looked intruded—he seemed to have gone from old to very old, very quickly.

His decline was evident in his ambivalence about doing one final film with Robert Redford. After several false starts, Redford had developed a script based on a book by Bill Bryson, *A Walk in the Woods*, that initially intrigued Paul, but he vacillated over committing himself, finally deciding that he was too old to do it. Redford was heartbroken. He very much wanted to make this movie with Paul, probably the last, but understood why it didn't happen. "Paul's been getting older fast," he said.

ON JANUARY 26, 2008, we celebrated Paul's eighty-third birthday, as we had celebrated his birthdays so many times over the years, with an intimate party in the Newman barn, but Paul was subdued and so was the party. Two days later, however, was Paul and Joanne's fiftieth wedding anniversary, and the party this time was cheerful and celebratory. Paul and Joanne reveled in interacting with the intimate group of family and old friends. The way they jointly cut the first piece of cake was a moment of happiness for all of us.

And then, putting aside the cake knife, Paul took both of Joanne's hands in his and drew her close to him. They looked at each other with intimate conspiracy, a look of endearment for those fifty years, and Paul said, "Joanna, being married to you has been the joy of my life."

BUT THERE WAS little laughter in the months that followed. Over the years Paul had exercised every morning in his gym, riding the stationary bike, lifting weights, working the Stairmaster, vigorously stretching—but now he was having trouble breathing and he felt drained of his usual energy. The playhouse announced that he had withdrawn from directing *Of Mice and Men*, and he canceled his two races at Lime Rock.

After tests revealed a lung condition that had to be rectified, Paul had surgery that resulted in a momentary reprieve from his malaise, but several months later, he was confronted with a forbidding new challenge—the onset of leukemia. He tried to maintain his spirit and his involvement with the events and people dear to him, but it was a losing battle. On the morning of a day we were scheduled to have lunch, this time at Mario's, Paul called to say he couldn't make it. He had gone to New York to have more tests. "I've been tested more than forty rats in a medical laboratory."

His voice was thin and scratchy. The man he was had been taken from him, and I hope deposited in some good place for safekeeping.

Paul's totem pole.

A major event had been scheduled for March 20, 2008, to celebrate the twentieth anniversary of the Hole in the Wall Gang Camp. It was to take place at New York's City Center, a 2,800-seat theater, and it was my responsibility to write and produce an entertainment for our contributors, an entertainment that would combine a select group of campers with some of the stars who had performed at the camp over those years: Carole King, Bernadette Peters, Joshua Bell, Harry Belafonte, Renee Zellweger, James Naughton, Bill Irwin, Nathan Lane, Christine Baranski, and Julia Roberts, among others.

Two days before the event, I went to see Paul in his New York apartment. In addition to his longtime housekeeper Cora, there was a nurse who brought Paul several medications and a special drink during the time I was there. Paul was anxious to participate in this important event, but we both knew that his role would have to be limited. We decided that he would only appear at the opening of the show. He would come in front of the curtain holding the hand of a little camper on either side of him. We wrote a few words of welcome and gratitude for him to say. Once in a while he hesitated, bowing his head, his eyes closed. But then he gathered himself and continued. I stayed for ten minutes at most.

He walked me to the door. He was not very steady. The nurse walked in back of us, concerned. I desperately wanted to say something funny or encouraging or disrespectful, hoping for a little of our customary badinage, but I wasn't up to it.

We faced each other at the door. "You think of anything more, you have my New York number."

"Sure," he said, and he tried to smile.

I stepped into the vestibule and rang for the elevator. Paul stayed in the doorway, the nurse behind him.

"Hotchnik," he said gently.

I looked at him and smiled.

He started to say something, thought about it, but all he said was, "Thanks."

"We'll give 'em a good show," I said. "We always do."

"Sure," Paul said, and he went back into the apartment. The nurse closed the door.

The elevator came. It descended slowly. I wished it would keep on going down and down.

ON THE DAY of the performance, at four o'clock in the afternoon, in the middle of the dress rehearsal for the seven o'clock show, I was called to the phone in the theater office. It was Paul.

"Hotch, I'm sorry, but listen, I can't do the show tonight. I hoped I could, I've insisted, but the doctors won't let me. I really want to be there—after all, twenty years, but . . ."

"That's all right, Paul, honestly. We will certainly miss you, but what the doctors say—"

"Yeah . . . yeah . . . the doctors . . ."

"We're videoing the show. I'll get it for you right away."

"Good luck, Hotchnik, break a leg." And he hung up.

I felt terrible. I had to go back to the auditorium and continue, but I couldn't move. I was alone in the office. I sat down and took a deep breath. I finally admitted to myself what I had desperately tried to avoid: Paul was dying. I couldn't get his sad words out of my head: "I can't do the show tonight."

Someone came for me and I forced myself to stand up and return to the auditorium. I knew my usual staff would provide solid support and I would do my best to put on a show that would, under these difficult circumstances, make Paul happy when he saw it on the video. But this was a night to commemorate Paul's great contribution and he would not be here to take a curtain call.

THE SHOW WENT very well. The children were enchanting, especially in a calypso number with Harry Belafonte and a funny sketch with Bill Irwin. The actors gave inspired performances. Toward the end of the show, in the middle of one of the numbers, two stagehands appeared, bringing onstage a beautifully carved totem pole. At its apex were a boy and a girl camper, her arm around his shoulders, and at its center a depiction of the Hole in the Wall dining hall surrounded by other camp vestiges. Along the base of the pole the word KISSES was embossed on one side and LOVE FROM ALL on the other.

James Naughton came onstage and told the audience, "Paul intended to present this totem pole to Hotch onstage tonight, but he asked me to read this: 'Hotch, this camp that we built is wonderful and this totem pole commemorates all you've contributed these twenty years. Put it in your backyard and enjoy it.' "

I brought the totem pole to Connecticut and erected it outside our breakfast-room windows, where I see it every morning.

*P*aul was increasingly in and out of the hospital all that winter. Late-night ambulances to Memorial Sloan-Kettering Cancer Center. Chemo. Nurses around the clock.

He still came to his office occasionally for brief spells, where he would answer letters, dictating his responses to his dedicated assistant, Darice Wirth. When I knew he was there, I'd come across the hall to see him. On one occasion, he was stretched out on his couch, covered with a thick blanket.

He motioned me to sit down on the side of the couch, facing him. He said he was cold all the time. He extended his hand to me. It was indeed very cold.

He asked about Virginia, whom he liked very much. "She's gentle and Southern like Joanne," he once said. "These Georgia ladies—must be the peach juice." He said he had just driven a few sedate laps around the course at Lime Rock in the Corvette that he had planned to race that summer. I found it hard to believe that in his condition he was even able to drive around the track, but racing had always brought out the best in him. He chided me for never racing my Corvette full-out. He gave me the name of the track manager at Lime Rock, said he would get permission for me to run the course. I reminded him that it was a '61 and that if I gave it full blast it would probably blow all its gaskets. And I would probably blow mine.

In the spring, with his gardens beginning to green, Paul had a promising resurgence. The doctors had been very concerned about his diminishing weight, but now he was pleased to report that his scale was showing an increase of a pound or two. When we had lunch he ordered desserts that featured fudge sauce and whipped cream. He talked about the possibility of competing in one race at Lime Rock, and maybe a few games of badminton with his usual group at the "Y." I was heartened to hear him talk like this, but, realistically, his frailty belied his wishes. I wanted to believe, however, that the new treatment his doctors had devised was going to slowly get him back on track.

It was a false hope. By the end of the summer his cancer had reasserted itself and he was forced back on the treadmill of critical ambulance runs between his house and the New York hospital. His weight diminished and so did hope.

*T*he first week of September 2008, I went to visit Paul at his house for the last time. He had stopped chemotherapy and all the other ineffectual curative procedures. He had fought hard against his cancer but he had run out of struggle and it was time to capitulate. Time for closure.

The night before my visit was sleepless hell. How would I say goodbye to this splendid man who had been such a presence in my life? I must not talk about what was happening or about to happen; no lugubriousness, that's not us. And yet, does he realize what his friendship has really meant to me? How much I admire the good things he accomplished? How his philosophy of living had affected how I live? And so many others? How I became imbued with his belief in reciprocity: the more you give to others, the more that good comes around to embrace you?

He had said that although when we started the camp he thought the children would be the beneficiaries, the truth was that we were the beneficiaries of the love and resolve of these children. So true.

No, none of that. It must be like all our other times.

Except, it would be the last time.

I dug my old Bahama jacket out of the closet, the one with "Man-O-War Cay, Abaco Bahama, Norman Albury Sailmakers" on the chest pocket. I thought Paul would get a kick out of seeing that. I drove my old Corvette along Long Lots Road onto North Avenue for the last time. I punched the code numbers into the electric-gate keypad. I parked the Vette outside the barn and, on impulse, went below and visited the underground area, the once-upon-a-time stables where we had mixed our first batch of salad dressing in the washtub.

I hadn't been down there since that faraway day. It was unchanged except for the presence of some gardening equipment. I looked at the dirt floor, the crumbled walls, the old cobwebby rafters, and shook my head at the audacity of our stirring up that brew down there.

I recalled the jolliness of our enterprise: the haphazard assembling of the ingredients; Paul's truculence at my inadequate waffling of the canoe paddle; the way we knocked in the corks (hitting an occasional thumb) and decorated the necks with blue ribbons.

I sat down on the seat of a garden tractor and thought about those early days when Paul's stubborn, uninformed convictions somehow managed to make the impossible possible. No, he would not contaminate his all-natural dressing with EDTA or anything else. Yes, our spaghetti sauce will have veggie chunks, and no, it will not be a mush like all the others. Those December pastrami lunches when we gave away every penny of our profits; that opening day when only a third of the sick children arrived and Paul was concerned that we were not going to succeed with the camp; Paul in the dining room, campers surrounding him, a beatific look on his face; the thousands of charities, the thousands of children, the incomparable movies, the humanitarian causes—all those trophies adorning the tree of his life.

I adjusted my face and left the stables and went up the steps leading to the kitchen. I never used the front door of the Newman house.

As I reached the top of the steps, I saw Paul, sitting outside the kitchen door in a shaded alcove. An open black umbrella lay on the ground beside him. Even though it was a mild day, Paul had a blanket around his shoulders. His face was very white against the dark wall behind him.

I waved to him as I approached and he nodded. He looked at the logo on my jacket pocket.

"How come I lose everything and you save everything?"

"You lost your jacket?"

"You probably sold it. Sit down."

I sat down beside the black umbrella. Paul kept looking at the logo. His eyes were alert but his face was a mask of putty.

"Let me ask you something." His voice was strong. "That festival—what was it called?"

"Guy Fawkes Day."

"Did you violate that pretty young woman with the sparklers?"

"She violated me."

"I knew it. The way she came up to you and asked you to light her sparklers."

"My tribute to Guy Fawkes."

"How many sparklers did she have?"

"I lost count."

"You lit all of them?"

"Yep."

"Good going." He leaned back and closed his eyes.

I sat quietly.

He opened his eyes and leaned forward. "I never played cricket again," he said.

"The girl with the red hair who stole your cricket cap . . ."

"What?"

"You remember. The team gave you a cricket cap . . ."

"Oh, yeah. That girl grabbed it."

"And?"

"I ran after her."

"And?"

"I caught up to her on the beach."

"And?"

"She gave me her bracelet made of feathers in exchange for my cap. Friends of hers came dancing along and she joined them and they all danced around me and sang songs while the fireworks made noise in the sky."

A nurse came out of the kitchen and gave Paul something to drink. He took a sip, made a face, and put it down.

"That Guy Fawkes Day—those Bahamians knew how to celebrate, didn't they?" I said.

"It seems all you and I ever did was celebrate one thing or another."

"Not the ice cream."

"What about the ice cream?"

"It was a flop."

"It was a great ice cream."

"It sure was. But it didn't sell."

"What were the names?"

"Obscene Vanilla Bean. Giddy-up Coffee. Mud Bath Chocolate."

"You always remember things, you tart," Paul said.

We sat for a while, silently remembering.

"I watched the video," Paul said. "Harry's something, isn't he?"

"He sure is."

Paul started to chant the song Belafonte had sung with the children. " 'Turn the World Around, Turn the World Around' . . . Harry . . . Harry's a fighter, you know. We were in the trenches together . . . He really did turn the world a tiny bit—in his quiet way."

"He performed at the camp with the kids three times."

"I remember."

"I'll never forget his singing 'There's a Hole in the Bottom of the Bucket' with Whoopi."

"Yeah. There's a hole in the bucket, all right. Did you ever see him dance when he was young? Calypso dance? Harry had it all."

"He said to tell you you're his hero."

"We need more."

"They're not easy to come by."

"Harry's hurting now, isn't he?" Paul said. "But he's still . . . Harry. 'Turn the World Around,' " softly mumbling it. "Harry's pure, you know? When he smiles that smile of his . . . pure."

So are you, I wanted to say. All these years, not a false move. You gave all you had. Nothing left now.

Paul stood up. "I'm running out of gas," he said. "Please hand me that umbrella."

I took the umbrella by its upturned handle, righted it, and passed it to Paul. He was only a few steps from the kitchen door. He placed the umbrella close over his head as he stepped from the shade into the sunshine.

"The sun hurts," he said.

I walked him to the door and opened it. He stepped into the kitchen and handed the umbrella to me. I closed it and leaned it against the doorjamb.

"I'll be in touch," I said.

"It's been a hell of a ride," he said, and he walked into the dark of the kitchen.

ACKNOWLEDGMENTS

Thanks to all who were helpful along the way: Claire Panke, Janet Durran, Timothy Hotchner, Roberta Pearson, David Kalman, Anna Harding, Robert Forrester, Charles Zunda, Tom Indoe, Charley Erickson, Mary Harper, Pam Papay, and assistant editor Ronit Feldman.

This is the fourth book I have written with Nan Talese as my editor, beginning with *Papa Hemingway*, and it has been a splendid and rewarding collaboration. Beyond editor, she is also one of my dearest friends, which doubles the pleasure of creating books with her.

I also wish to toss a bouquet to my wife, Virginia, for how much she helped me accommodate the emotional content of this book—this in addition to all her other virtues.

PHOTO CREDITS

A NOTE ABOUT THE TYPE

This book has been typeset in Monotype Garamond, a version of the original Garamond first introduced in 1541. This beautiful, classic font has been a standard among book designers and printers for more than four hundred years. While opinion varies as to the role that typecutter Claude Garamond played in the development of the typeface that bears his name, there is no doubt that this font had great influence on the evolution of other typefaces from the sixteenth century to the present.